RAIN OF ABUNDANCE

RAIN OF ABUNDANCE

Peter Oluwole

Contact

+1317-748-5778

+1317-701-9991

christspeminternational@gmail.com

Contents

Introduction

Lack is the opposite of abundance. Dryness or drought is the opposite of rain. Lack and dryness are synonymous. They have in them the spirits of poverty, penury, and pity. On the other hand, rain and abundance signify prosperity. When rain falls, farmers are happy because their farmland will be nourished and hope of a bumper harvest is assured.

On that note, I welcome you to your season of abundance. This realm of abundance will mark the end of your suffering and challenges. In this realm, a flood of favor, blessings, and God's abiding faithfulness are assured.

You have toiled enough. Your prayers have ascended to heaven. God has answered your prayers. The seasons of drought and lack are over in your life. This book will show you how to be a partaker of the rain of abundance. There are diverse patterns of rain on Earth. Drizzling, shower, and torrential downpour. These also apply to spiritual blessings; some come in drizzling forms. Some come with a greater force, flooding your surroundings.

Therefore, just as blessings are experienced in different levels, so does abundance manifest in various forms too. There are blessings that fall gently like a drizzle, providing for our basic needs and ensuring survival. Other blessings pour down with greater intensity, nourishing not only our immediate family but also extending their reach to our kin.

Moreover, there are blessings akin to a downpour, where the abundance bestowed upon us becomes a cascade that can sustain an entire city. These blessings transform us into conduits of divine provision, enabling us to bring forth a deluge of blessings upon others, transcending boundaries and quenching the thirst of many.

Today, dear readers, I am thrilled to unveil an extraordinary order of blessings—the Rain of Abundance. This sacred downpour of blessings elevates you beyond the limitations of ordinary provision, propelling you into the realm of exceptional favor. With each droplet that touches your life, you will witness a transformation—a metamorphosis that turns you into a great nation, capable of not only feeding the nations of the world but also lending a helping hand to those in need.

As the Rain of Abundance pours over you, its life-giving waters will drench your name in greatness. No longer will you remain a local champion confined to the corner shop; instead, you will become a global brand, recognized and revered by leading financial institutions across the globe.

Under the guidance of the Holy Spirit, I have been inspired to share this message, proclaiming your imminent journey into the realm of extraordinary blessings. Within this realm, curses lose their power, and the forces of evil are rendered impotent, both in your life and in the lives of your descendants.

Prepare yourself to embrace the destiny of a great nation, anointed with unprecedented speed and abundance. As you immerse yourself in the pages of this book, I encourage you to read, pray, and meditate, for it is through these practices that you will fully receive the downpour of blessings that awaits you.

1.

SAY NO TO DROUGHT & DRYNESS

I am the LORD thy God, which brought thee out of the land of Egypt: open thy mouth wide, and I will fill it.

Psalm 81:10

Drought is defined as a long period when there is little or no rain. It is a condition that occurs when there is a prolonged period of insufficient rainfall, resulting in barren landscapes. This is a period of sorrow. It is a period when nothing is working. Drought and dryness symbolize times of lack, emptiness, and sorrow.

Drought and dryness are states of deprivation, scarcity, and desolation. Financial difficulties, broken relationships, unfulfilled dreams, and a lack of purpose can leave people feeling empty, and devoid of hope.

There are different dimensions of drought and dryness: Season of Dryness; Season of Bareness; Season of Lack; Season of Frustration; Season of Disappointment; Season of Delay;

Financial Drought & Dryness; Marital Drought & Dryness; Spiritual Drought & Dryness, etc.

All these dimensions can refer to periods in the lives of people when they feel spiritually drained and disconnected from God. It can manifest as a lack of spiritual growth, diminished passion for worship, and a sense of spiritual emptiness.

Most people who are ignorant of their redemptive rights might experience this season as they thread the path of unfruitfulness and lack of productivity. Their careers, relationships, creativity, or personal growth are stunted.

A season of drought and dryness will lead to feelings of frustration, anxiety, and a sense of helplessness. It can also be marked by setbacks, obstacles, and unfulfilled expectations.

Open Your Mouth

In case you find yourself stuck in the arena of dryness and drought, there is a way out. You need to take practical steps to exit this path of pity. A pity party will not save you. Begging the enemies that have locked you down in this cage of despair will not solve the issue. The only way out is to use the weapon of the word. You must take action!

You must open your mouth to declare your victory. You must command your deliverance. In the face of dryness and sorrow, it is imperative that we open our mouths and command our deliverance. Throughout the Scriptures, we find numerous examples of individuals who found themselves in desolate situations but chose to speak words of faith, invoking the power of God to intervene. Just as God commanded the earth to bring forth life in the beginning, we too possess the ability to speak life into our circumstances.

Through the power of our words, aligned with God's promises, we can bring about transformation and experience a season of abundance and flourishing. Let us open our mouths, speak with faith, and trust in the goodness and faithfulness of our Heavenly Father. Say no to drought and dryness, and step into a life filled with the refreshing rain of God's blessings.

Here are ways to command victory into your life when faced with drought and dryness:

1. Speak with Authority: When we are faced with adversity, we must remember that we have been given authority through Jesus Christ. Matthew 28:18 reminds us that Jesus has been given all authority in heaven and on earth. As His followers, we can boldly declare His promises over our lives and situations. Our words carry power when spoken with faith and aligned with the will of God.
2. Declare God's Promises: The Bible is filled with promises that assure us of God's faithfulness, provision, and restoration. In times of drought and dryness, we need to meditate on these promises, internalize them, and boldly declare them over our lives. For example, Isaiah 41:10 states, "So do not fear, for I am with you; do not be dismayed, for I am your God. I will strengthen you and help you; I will uphold you with my righteous right hand." When we speak these promises, we activate God's power to work on our behalf.
3. Cultivate a Heart of Gratitude: Gratitude is a powerful tool to combat dryness and sorrow. Even in the midst of challenging circumstances, we can choose to be thankful for the blessings we have received. When we cultivate a heart of gratitude, our focus shifts from lack to

abundance, from sorrow to joy. Expressing gratitude opens the door for God's provision and restoration to flow into our lives.

Prayers

1. I command every dry season in my life to come to an end. Let the rain of your blessings and abundance begin to fall upon me now!
2. Lord Jesus, you have given me authority over all the works of the enemy. I take a stand against every spirit of drought and dryness that has plagued my life. I decree fruitfulness.
3. By the authority in the name of Jesus, I command dryness and drought to be uprooted and destroyed. Let the rivers of living water flow into every area of my life and bring forth fruitfulness and prosperity.
4. Heavenly Father, I declare your promises over my life. Your Word says in Jeremiah 17:7-8 that blessed is the man who trusts in you and whose hope is in You. I choose to put my trust in you, and I declare that I am like a tree planted by the waters, always green and fruitful. Every dry and barren area of my life is transformed by your promises and provision in Jesus' name.
5. Heavenly Father, I rebuke every spirit of frustration, anxiety, and helplessness that has come with the season of drought and dryness. I declare that I am filled with your peace that surpasses all understanding in Jesus' name.
6. Lord, I command every financial drought and dryness in

my life to be broken. I declare that you arc my provider in Jesus' name.

7. Heavenly Father, I command every delay and disappointment in my life to be overturned. I declare that Your timing is perfect, and you make all things beautiful in your time in Jesus' name.
8. Lord, I declare that I am stepping out of the dryness and into the rain of your blessings in Jesus' name.
9. My head rejects dryness. I will continually ever work in the realm of fruitfulness and greatness in Jesus' name.
10. In the name of Jesus, my life will forever be refreshed with God's abiding favour and grace. Testimonies shall not depart from my mouth.

2.

GOD OF ABUNDANCE

And you, be ye fruitful, and multiply; bring forth abundantly in the earth, and multiply therein.

Genesis 9:7

It gives me great pleasure to introduce you to the God of abundance. He is the one who commands rain of abundance to fall on his people. Rain of abundance brings abundant blessings and goodness.

Abundance represents plentiful, great increase, surplus, overflowing, enough, much, large amount, prosperity, riches, wealth, prosperous, blooming, bright, etc.

But my God shall supply all your need according to his riches in glory by Christ Jesus.
Philippians 4:19

The LORD is my shepherd; I shall not want. He maketh me to lie down in green pastures: he leadeth me beside the still waters.

He restoreth my soul: he leadeth me in the paths of righteousness for his name's sake.
Yea, though I walk through the valley of the shadow of death, I will fear no evil: for thou art with me; thy rod and thy staff they comfort me. Thou preparest a table before me in the presence of mine enemies: thou anointest my head with oil; my cup runneth over.
Surely goodness and mercy shall follow me all the days of my life: and I will dwell in the house of the LORD forever.

Psalms 23:1 – 6

Wait! There is more. We serve the God of abundant favour, mercy, help, provision and kindness.

But the meek shall inherit the earth; and shall delight themselves in the abundance of peace.

Psalms 37:11

For the LORD hath chosen Zion; he hath desired it feor his habitation. This is my rest for ever: here will I dwell; for I have desired it. I will abundantly bless her provision: I will satisfy her poor with bread.

Psalms 132:13-15

And you, be ye fruitful, and multiply; bring forth abundantly in the earth, and multiply therein.

Genesis 9:7

You will bring forth abundance in the name of Jesus. You will receive abundant ideas. You will show forth abundance in all areas. You will manifest abundance. You will have evidence of abundance in Jesus' name. You will receive results of abundance. You will possess abundance. You will operate in the realm of abundance in Jesus' name.

Thou shalt increase my greatness, and comfort me on every side.
Psalms 71:21

I command that you will:

- Receive abundant comfort.
- Receive abundant mercy.
- Receive abundant help.
- Receive abundant grace.
- Receive abundant favour.
- Receive abundant blessings.

In Jesus' name

They shall call the people unto the mountain; there they shall offer sacrifices of righteousness: for they shall suck of the abundance of the seas, and of treasures hid in the sand.
Deuteronomy 33:19

Again, I command that you will receive abundant provision and treasures in Jesus' name.

And to know the love of Christ, which passeth knowledge, that ye might be filled with all the fulness of God.
Now unto him that is able to do exceeding abundantly above

all that we ask or think, according to the power that worketh in us,
Unto him be glory in the church by Christ Jesus throughout all ages, world without end. Amen.
Ephesians 3:19-21

I pray for you that, the power of God for abundance in all areas shall fall upon you now in Jesus' name. Oil of abundance shall fall upon you in Jesus' name. Grace for abundance in all areas shall fall upon you now in Jesus' name.

But Jesus said unto them, They need not depart; give ye them to eat. And they say unto him, We have here but five loaves, and two fishes. He said, Bring them hither to me. And he commanded the multitude to sit down on the grass, and took the five loaves, and the two fishes, and looking up to heaven, he blessed, and brake, and gave the loaves to his disciples, and the disciples to the multitude. And they did all eat, and were filled: and they took up of the fragments that remained twelve baskets full. And they that had eaten were about five thousand men, beside women and children.
***Matthew* 14:16-21**

Prayer

1. Heavenly Father, I thank you for being the God of abundance. I praise you for your overflowing blessings and goodness in my life.
2. In the name of Jesus, I decree divine abundance for all my needs and desires.
3. I stand on your promises as written in your word. I claim

the abundance that you have promised in Genesis 9:7, that I may be fruitful and multiply in all areas of my life in Jesus' name.

4. Lord, I trust in your unfailing provision as stated in Philippians 4:19. I believe that you will supply all my needs according to your riches in glory through Christ Jesus in Jesus' name
5. I declare that I dwell in your abundance, and I shall not want in Jesus' name.
6. As stated in Psalms 23, I rest in your green pastures and beside still waters. You lead me in righteousness, and your goodness and mercy follow me all the days of my life.
7. Lord, I receive your abundant favour, mercy, help, provision, and kindness as mentioned in your word. I know that you have chosen me, and I am satisfied with your abundant blessings in Jesus' name.
8. In Jesus name, I walk in the abundance of peace, joy and prosperity.
9. My Father and my God, I decree that I will have more than enough to meet my needs and bless others around the world in Jesus' name.
10. Heavenly Father, I pray that you open my spiritual eyes to see the abundance and opportunities all around me.

3.

EXCEPTIONAL BLESSINGS

And the floors shall be full of wheat, and the vats shall overflow with wine and oil.

Joel 2:24

The online dictionary defines blessing as God's favour and protection. It can also be protection. The synonyms are advantage, benefit, help, boon, good thing, Godsent, gift, convenience, bonus, plus point, added attraction, additional benefit, extra, added extra, luck, good fortune, windfall, gain, profit, virtue, bounty, plus, perk, etc.

The above are dictionary definitions. Now, let us look at the Bible's perspective on blessings:

Now the LORD had said unto Abram, Get thee out of thy country, and from thy kindred, and from thy father's house, unto a land that I will shew thee:
And I will make of thee a great nation, and I will bless thee, and make thy name great; and thou shalt be a blessing:
And I will bless them that bless thee, and curse him that

curseth thee: and in thee shall all families of the earth be blessed.

Genesis 12:1-3

The kinds of blessings that God has in mind for his people are exceptional blessings. These kinds of blessings were the ones bestowed on Abraham in the scripture quoted above. In that realm of blessing, God made Abraham a great nation. He was blessed and his name was made great. Since then, he has been a blessing to all nations of the earth.

Not only that, as soon as Abraham received God's blessings, all his enemies automatically become God's enemies. Those who blessed him were blessed, and through him, all families of the earth are being blessed!

The blessing of the LORD, it maketh rich, and he addeth no sorrow with it.

Proverbs 10:22

Exceptional blessing is:

- Rain of abundance
- God's favor
- Blessings without sorrow
- Blessings without tragedy
- Blessings without hardship
- Blessings without difficulties
- Blessings without backwardness
- Blessings without setback
- Blessings without sickness
- Blessings without premature death

- Blessings without affliction
- Blessings without tragedy
- Blessings without loses
- Blessings without failure

For thou hast made him most blessed forever: thou hast made him exceeding glad with thy countenance.
Psalms 21:6

Exceptional blessing is:

- Special blessings from above
- Supernatural blessings that activate favour
- Blessings that terminate curses and spells
- Favour among favour
- That which changes your name to highly favoured
- About the release of undeserved kindness towards the victim (Declare after me: I shall be a candidate of supernatural blessings in Jesus' name)
- Unmerited goodness
- Prosperity without sorrow
- The mighty hands that open doors of unexpected progress
- The acceptance without qualification
- That which gives access to breakthrough and turnaround
- That which gives you justification without proof
- Special blessings: released harvest without hard labour.
- Blessings that turn enchantment and divination to blessings

I decree that you will enter your realm of special blessings and the blessings will terminate curses and spell in your life in Jesus' name. In the name of Jesus, you are blessed as from today than ever before.

And I will make them and the places round about my hill a blessing; and I will cause the shower to come down in his season; there shall be showers of blessing.
And the tree of the field shall yield her fruit, and the earth shall yield her increase, and they shall be safe in their land, and shall know that I am the LORD, when I have broken the bands of their yoke, and delivered them out of the hand of those that served themselves of them.
And they shall no more be a prey to the heathen, neither shall the beast of the land devour them; but they shall dwell safely, and none shall make them afraid.

Ezekiel 34:26 -28

For thou, LORD, wilt bless the righteous; with favour wilt thou compass him as with a shield.

Psalm 5:12

God loves you. You are his favourite. He will shower you with blessings and favour. You will not miss your way in Jesus' name.

And the Lord shall guide thee continually, and satisfy thy soul in drought, and make fat thy bones: and thou shalt be like a watered garden, and like a spring of water, whose waters fail not.

Isaiah 58:11

Prayers

1. I receive showers of blessings.
2. I receive the rain of blessings.
3. The dews of blessings will fall on me.
4. The favour of God with divine security is mine in Jesus' name.
5. In my marital life, I shall be blessed.
6. I am financially blessed.
7. Materially, I shall be blessed in Jesus' name.
8. Spiritually, I shall be blessed in Jesus' name.

In the name of Jesus

- I will be spiritually fit
- I shall be spiritually strong and be stronger
- I shall be spiritually powerful
- my prayer life is stable
- my study life is balanced
- my spiritual growth shall increase

10. In the name of Jesus, my testimony will be that of exceptional blessings in Jesus name.

4.

BENEFITS OF EXCEPTIONAL BLESSINGS

And the angel of the LORD called unto Abraham out of heaven the second time, And said, By myself have I sworn, saith the LORD, for because thou hast done this thing, and hast not withheld thy son, thine only son: That in blessing I will bless thee, and in multiplying I will multiply thy seed as the stars of the heaven, and as the sand which is upon the sea shore; and thy seed shall possess the gate of his enemies; And in thy seed shall all the nations of the earth be blessed; because thou hast obeyed my voice.

Genesis 22:15-18

Exceptional blessings are all-encompassing. They come to the recipients of the blessings in large quantities. No half measures. Here are features of what exceptional blessings command:

Exceptional Blessings Command Long Life

With long life will I satisfy him, and shew him my salvation
Psalms 91:16

This is a promise from God. Exceptional blessings command long life. Let's look at the fulfillment of God's exceptional blessing of long life, as given to Abraham:

And these are the days of the years of Abraham's life which he lived, an hundred threescore and fifteen years.
Then Abraham gave up the ghost, and died in a good old age, an old man, and full of years; and was gathered to his people.
Genesis 25:7-8

Isaac also experienced the fulfillment of God's promises in respect of the package of long life:

And the days of Isaac were an hundred and fourscore years. And Isaac gave up the ghost, and died, and was gathered unto his people, being old and full of days: and his sons Esau and Jacob buried him.
Genesis 35:28-29

Moses received the blessings of God. He died at the age of 120 years.

And Moses was an hundred and twenty years old when he died: his eye was not dim, nor his natural force abated.
Deuteronomy 34:7

Exceptional Blessings Command both Physical Strength and Spiritual Strength

The exceptional blessing is two in one package – You 'buy one and get one free'! You get both spiritual and physical blessings for the price of one. Your strengths physically and spiritually are replenished.

And such as do wickedly against the covenant shall he corrupt by flatteries: but the people that do know their God shall be strong, and do exploits.

Daniel 11:32

Hast thou not known? hast thou not heard, that the everlasting God, the LORD, the Creator of the ends of the earth, fainteth not, neither is weary? there is no searching of his understanding.
He giveth power to the faint; and to them that have no might he increaseth strength.
Even the youths shall faint and be weary, and the young men shall utterly fall:
But they that wait upon the LORD shall renew their strength; they shall mount up with wings as eagles; they shall run, and not be weary; and they shall walk, and not faint.

Isaiah 40:28-31

Exceptional Blessings Command Settlement and Stability

Settlement and stability are certain when God bestows exceptional blessings on you. You are free from the devil's encumbrances.

In Genesis 22, 23, and 24, Abraham experienced divine settlement and stability. In 1 King 2:12, we read the account of

Solomon – how he experienced settlement and stability in his kingdom:

Then sat Solomon upon the throne of David his father; and his kingdom was established greatly.
1 Kings 2:12

But the God of all grace, who hath called us unto his eternal glory by Christ Jesus, after that ye have suffered a while, make you perfect, stablish, strengthen, settle you.
1 Peter 5:10

Similarly, when God's exceptional blessings descend on you, you will experience settlement and stability. This settlement and stability will give you results that will stabilize your life. You will enjoy marital settlement, financial settlement, emotional settlement, etc.

Cry to God for this kind of blessing. Don't miss it. It will make life easy for you.

Exceptional Blessings Command Restoration

All that you may have lost are restored when you encounter exceptional blessings. You are moving from one glory to another glory. For instance, Job was restored after losing all that he had.

Then all his brothers, all his sisters, and all those who had been his acquaintances before, came to him and ate food with him in his house; and they consoled him and comforted him for all the adversity that the LORD had brought upon him. Each one gave him a piece of silver and each a ring of gold. Now the

LORD blessed the latter days of Job more than his beginning; for he had fourteen thousand sheep, six thousand camels, one thousand yoke of oxen, and one thousand female donkeys.

Job 42:11-12 NKJV

In the name of Jesus, I command your great restoration.

Therefore, all they that devour thee shall be devoured; and all thine adversaries, every one of them, shall go into captivity; and they that spoil thee shall be a spoil, and all that prey upon thee will I give for a prey.

For I will restore health unto thee, and I will heal thee of thy wounds, saith the LORD; because they called thee an Outcast, saying, This is Zion, whom no man seeketh after.

Thus saith the LORD; Behold, I will bring again the captivity of Jacob's tents, and have mercy on his dwelling places; and the city shall be builded upon her own heap, and the palace shall remain after the manner thereof.

And out of them shall proceed thanksgiving and the voice of them that make merry: and I will multiply them, and they shall not be few; I will also glorify them, and they shall not be small.

Their children also shall be as aforetime, and their congregation shall be established before me, and I will punish all that oppress them.

And their nobles shall be of themselves, and their governor shall proceed from the midst of them; and I will cause him to draw near, and he shall approach unto me: for who is this that engaged his heart to approach unto me? saith the LORD.

And ye shall be my people, and I will be your God.

Behold, the whirlwind of the LORD goeth forth with fury, a continuing whirlwind: it shall fall with pain upon the head of the wicked.

The fierce anger of the LORD shall not return, until he have done it, and until he have performed the intents of his heart: in the latter days ye shall consider it.

Jeremiah 30: 16-24

John answered and said, A man can receive nothing, except it be given him from heaven.

John 3:27

Prayers

1. Thank you, father, for my heritage of exceptional blessings.
2. I receive anointing for exceptional blessings.
3. Exceptional blessings rest upon me now in the name of Jesus Christ.
4. The mercy of God search out my blessings for restoration in Jesus' name.
5. O Heavens, open upon my glory for manifestation in Jesus' name.
6. My glory and blessing, arise, and shine in Jesus' name
7. My blessings, kept in any captivity or any bondage, escape now in Jesus' name.
8. Family altar holding my blessing down, scatter by fire in Jesus' name.
9. Family darkness covering my blessings, fade away now in Jesus' name.
10. I receive grace for blessings that transcend generations in Jesus' name.

11. I become the father of many nations in Jesus' name.
12. I lend to nations in Jesus' name.

5.

UNDERSTANDING HOW TO TRIGGER THE RAIN OF ABUNDANCE

Blessed is the man that trusteth in the LORD, and whose hope the LORD is. For he shall be as a tree planted by the waters, and that spreadeth out her roots by the river, and shall not see when heat cometh, but her leaf shall be green; and shall not be careful in the year of drought, neither shall cease from yielding fruit.

Jeremiah 17:7-8

There are dimensions to God's exceptional blessings and rain of abundance. They are triggered by:

Trusting In God

Blessed is the man that trusteth in the LORD, and whose hope the LORD is. For he shall be as a tree planted by the waters, and

that spreadeth out her roots by the river, and shall not see when heat cometh, but her leaf shall be green; and shall not be careful in the year of drought, neither shall cease from yielding fruit.
***Jeremiah* 17:7-8**

You can trigger exceptional blessings by trusting in God with strong confidence. This means that you need to hold on to his promises in spite of challenges and situations that are in variance to God's plan and purpose for your life.

Giving God Quality Service

And ye shall serve the LORD *your* God, *and he shall bless thy bread, and thy water; and I will take sickness away from the midst of thee. There shall nothing cast their young, nor be barren, in thy land: the number of thy days I will fulfill*
Exodus 23:25-26

Give God quality service. You can touch God's heart through your service in his kingdom. Serve with your gifts.

Serve with your heart, don't grumble.
Give all that you have.
Serve with your skill.
Serve with your time.
Serve with your money.
Serve with your possession.
Always look for opportunities to serve God.

Releasing Your Isaac unto God

And said, By myself have I sworn, saith the LORD, *for because*

thou hast done this thing, and hast not withheld thy son, thine only son:
That in blessing I will bless thee, and in multiplying I will multiply thy seed as the stars of the heaven, and as the sand which is upon the sea shore; and thy seed shall possess the gate of his enemies; And in thy seed shall all the nations of the earth be blessed; because thou hast obeyed my voice.
Genesis 22:16-18

Give God your Isaac. Your Isaac is that thing that is occupying God's position in your life. It is that thing contending with God's space in your life.

Your Isaac may be your husband, wife, children, work, money, body, etc. Give them all to God. He would replace them with supernatural blessings.

Obeying God's Instruction

And all these blessings shall come on thee, and overtake thee, if thou shalt hearken unto the voice of the LORD thy God Blessed shalt thou be in the city, and blessed shalt thou be in the field.
Deuteronomy 28:2-3

You need to obey God's instruction(s) at every point in time. God will be speaking to you through your mind, conscience, and through his word (Bible).

Not only that, you need to also submit yourself to your spouse. Let them serve as a guide unto you so that you don't go astray.

Submitting yourselves one to another in the fear of God. Wives, submit yourselves unto your own husbands, as unto the Lord. For the husband is the head of the wife, even as Christ is the head of the church: and he is the saviour of the body. Therefore, as the church is subject unto Christ, so let the wives be to their own husbands in everything. Husbands, love your wives, even as Christ also loved the church, and gave himself for it;

Ephesians 5:21-25

If you are truly obedient to God, you need to also obey Godly instructions from your God-ordained prophets.

And they rose early in the morning, and went forth into the wilderness of Tekoa: and as they went forth, Jehoshaphat stood and said, Hear me, O Judah, and ye inhabitants of Jerusalem; Believe in the LORD your God, so shall ye be established; believe his prophets, so shall ye prosper.

2 Chronicles 20:20

He that receiveth a prophet in the name of a prophet shall receive a prophet's reward; and he that receiveth a righteous man in the name of a righteous man shall receive a righteous man's reward.

Matthew 10:41

Retreating for Divine Encounter

And Jacob was left alone; and there wrestled a man with him until the breaking of the day. And when he saw that he prevailed not against him, he touched the hollow of his thigh;

and the hollow of Jacob's thigh was out of joint, as he wrestled with him.
And he said, Let me go, for the day breaketh. And he said, I will not let thee go, except thou bless me. And he said unto him, What is thy name? And he said, Jacob.And he said, Thy name shall be called no more Jacob, but Israel: for as a prince hast thou power with God and with men, and hast prevailed.
And Jacob asked him, and said, Tell me, I pray thee, thy name. And he said, Wherefore is it that thou dost ask after my name? And he blessed him there.

Genesis 32:24- 29

Like Jacob, you need to have regular retreats in order to have divine encounters for your exceptional blessings.

Demanding for Rain of Abundance and Blessings

And Jabez was more honourable than his brethren: and his mother called his name Jabez, saying, Because I bare him with sorrow.
And Jabez called on the God of Israel, saying, Oh that thou wouldest bless me indeed, and enlarge my coast, and that thine hand might be with me, and that thou wouldest keep me from evil, that it may not grieve me! And God granted him that which he requested.

***1 Chronicles* 4:9-10**

Jabez was challenged but he was determined and demanded it. You need to be determined to get your exceptional blessings.

Prayers

1. Father, release my blessings in Jesus' name.
2. My father, release great help and helper unto me in Jesus' name.
3. My Lord, release my blessings in Jesus' name.
4. My Lord and Savior, release great help and helper unto me in Jesus' name
5. Heaven, let my rain of abundance come speedily in Jesus' name.
6. In Jesus name, let the power of your blood transit me into your realm of blessings.
7. I decree in Jesus' name, that failure and drought will never come my way in Jesus' name.
8. Father, let your hand take me away from the pit and move me into the palace in Jesus' name.
9. I demand my rain of abundance right now in Jesus' name.
10. My rain of abundance, come down now. My rain of abundance, come upon me now. My rain of abundance, overflow me now in Jesus' name.

6.

DESTROYING THE ALTAR OF NEGATIVE STATEMENTS (CURSES & SPELL) THAT CAN STOP THE RAIN OF ABUNDANCE

Blotting out the handwriting of ordinances that was against us, which was contrary to us, and took it out of the way, nailing it to his cross; And having spoiled principalities and powers, he made a shew of them openly, triumphing over them in it.

Colossians 2:14-25

What are negative words and prayers? These are dark words or prayers ...

- inspired by the enemies
- said with satanic anointing
- ungodly words or prayers
- occult words or prayers

- said with satanic fasting (Acts 16)
- witchcraft prayers standing against one's blessing
- offered by Satanists
- of wicked utterances
- contrary to the Bible
- aimed to destroy
- targeted to cause havoc or destruction

Death and life are in the power of tongue
Proverbs 18:21

Let us look at curses. In the scriptures, curses are in the armoury of the enemies. There are people around whose profession is to curse. Balak was hired by Balaam to help him curse the people of Israel.

And the ass saw the angel of the Lord standing in the way, and his sword drawn in his hand: and the ass turned aside out of the way, and went into the field: and Balaam smote the ass, to turn her into the way.
Number 22:23

Goliath Cursed David

And the Philistine said unto David, [Am] I a dog, that thou comest to me with staves? And the Philistine cursed David by his gods
1 Samuel 17:43

However, when Goliath cursed David, he responded aggressively. He neutralized the curses by speaking back.

Curses are too rampant in our environment these days. The trouble with curses is that they go directly to the root of the life of the affected person. That is the reason you need to emulate David by reacting aggressively to curses using the word of God.

Incantations/Demonic Recitation/Chant

These are invitations to demonic forces to cause harm. It can be night chanting; chanting on one leg; chanting on evil mats; chanting on their knees, etc.

To neutralize it, read Isaiah 8:9–10, "... *Take counsel together, and it shall come to nought; speak the word, and it shall not stand: for God is with us.*"

Words Spoken in Anger

A soft answer turneth away wrath: but grievous words stir up anger.

Proverbs 15:1

For the wrath of man worketh not the righteousness of God

James 1:20

Angry words and bad words are backed up by bad spirits to wreak havoc. Please stop going into unnecessary arguments, especially with men of God. Anyone filled with the Holy Ghost should avoid hot verbal exchange of words with people.

A soft answer turns away wrath.
Proverbs 15:1

Evil Desire

And the Lord said, Simon, Simon, behold, Satan hath desired [to have] you, that he may sift [you] as wheat
Luke 22:31

This is the desire of the enemies to destroy.

Satanic Report

Curses can take the form of satanic reports, e.g., Balak vs Balaam. When somebody goes to a witch doctor or herbalist or an evil prophet or occult people to report a person, they will open an evil case file on the person.

Careless Abuses for Playful Purposes

These can be unnecessary jesting, mimicking, side comments, etc.

False Swearing

But I say unto you, Swear not at all; neither by heaven; for it is God's throne: 35 Nor by the earth; for it is his footstool: neither by Jerusalem; for it is the city of the great King. 36 Neither shalt thou swear by thy head, because thou canst not make one hair white or black.
Mathew 5:34–36

When things happen, the people involved are gathered to swear to prove their innocence. When you do that, you are offering dark prayers against your life. Don't swear falsely!

Demonic Prophecies

Many have gone to places to acquire evil prophecies before their new birth and after. Many strange hands have been laid upon many people and strange prayers said. Many have accepted dark prayers through this medium.

Word of Divination and Enchanting

This can be speaking negative words to the sun, moon, star, or any creature against someone.

Charms, Spells & Spitting

These turn people's lives into dustbins or dungeons.

SPECIALISTS IN DARK PRAYERS

Stand now with thine enchantments, and with the multitude of thy sorceries, wherein thou hast laboured from thy youth; if so be thou shalt be able to profit, if so be thou mayest prevail. Thou art wearied in the multitude of thy counsels. Let now the astrologers, the stargazers, the monthly prognosticators, stand up, and save thee from [these things] that shall come upon thee.

Isaiah 47:12-13

- Enchanters
- Sorcerers

- Astrologers: they peruse the heavens
- Star gazers: they gaze into the stars
- Monthly prognosticators

EFFECTS OF NEGATIVE STATEMENTS

1. It causes sudden destruction to its victims
2. It is a weapon of injury from the camp of the enemies
3. It brings sudden or untimely death
4. Negative words or prayers bring confusion, distraction, or frustration
5. It is the killer of a glorious destiny
6. It can put off the shine the light of the victim
7. It is an arrow of failure, tragedy, havoc, etc.
8. It is a spiritual virus of sicknesses or diseases
9. It operates like a devourer and waster
10. It kills suddenly
11. It pushes good things away
12. It gives room for repeated attacks
13. It causes dream manipulation and defilement

Surely there is no enchantment against Jacob, neither is there any divination against Israel: according to this time it shall be said of Jacob and of Israel,"

***Number* 23:23**

As the bird by wandering, as the swallow by flying, so the curse causeless shall not come

***Proverbs* 26:2**

It is my prayer for you that you will receive blessings that have divine protection, divine preservation, divine security, divine peace and joy, kindness and compassion.

Prayers

1. Negative prayers targeted against my destiny, backfire in Jesus' name
2. Negative utterances targeted against my destiny, backfire in Jesus' name
3. Negative jesting targeted against my destiny, backfire in Jesus' name
4. Negative prophecies targeted against my destiny, backfire in Jesus' name
5. Negative predictions targeted against my destiny, backfire in Jesus' name
6. Negative recitation targeted against my destiny, backfire in Jesus' name
7. Negative pronouncements targeted against my destiny, backfire in Jesus' name
8. Negative sounds targeted against my destiny, backfire in Jesus' name
9. Negative speaking targeted against my destiny, backfire in Jesus
10. Negative news targeted against my destiny, backfire in Jesus' name
11. Sorcerers raining dark prayers against my life, let their prayers backfire in the name of Jesus.
12. Astrologers raining dark prayers against my life, let their prayers backfire in the name of Jesus.

13. Star gazers raining dark prayers against my life, let their prayers backfire in the name of Jesus.
14. Monthly prognosticators raining dark prayers against my life, let their prayers backfire in the name of Jesus.

7.

OPERATING IN THE REALM OF EXCEPTIONAL GRACE

And the king loved Esther above all the women, and she obtained grace and favour in his sight more than all the virgins; so that he set the royal crown upon her head, and made her queen instead of Vashti.

Esther 2:17

When there is a rain of abundance, grace is at work. What is grace? Grace is God's given ability to do the unusual. Grace is doing things with ease. Grace makes you function without struggles. Grace is the divine ability to start and complete a God-given task in spite of opposition, obstacles, and adversity.

Grace is an unmerited favor. It is needed for progress, victory, and success for a brighter and better future. However, it has one major rival – sin. In a life where sin increases, grace diminishes. Where grace increases, the tendency to sin will reduce. Also, pride reduces grace. Jeremiah 9: 23, 24.

The grace of God must not be taken for granted. You can ask

God to increase your grace deposit – "And God is able to make all grace abound."

If you embark on an assignment above your grace, you will crash. Don't compare your grace with the grace of your friends. Everyone has a measure of grace. Don't envy anyone or be jealous. Celebrate grace. The grace you don't celebrate will not benefit you.

Grace makes you rise again when you fall. Grace strengthens and keeps you humble. Through grace, God uses our very limited strength & resources to do the impossible. Grace can be accessed in varying measures, to some people, grace may be unavailable, to some, only a little, while some will have it in abundance, and for some others; grace will outweigh their needs.

If you want to access extreme levels of grace, do not frustrate God's grace that is currently available for you. Grace makes you to excel far above your natural ability.

Don't become a storage tower of grace but rather, be a channel of grace. Use grace for the purpose for which it was given to you. Grace sets you on the path of success, and journeys with you until you achieve your goals. Grace makes you excel in spite of your human weakness.

Grace makes you to focus on the goodness and the faithfulness of God rather than your efforts and ability. Christianity is a journey of grace and we can grow in grace on a daily basis. God's grace is given to us at different times for different needs.

Our salvation is by grace and not by our works. (Ephesians 2:8). We must keep asking for grace and appreciating the grace of God daily. To make Heaven is by God's grace. Grace is doing things with ease. I decree that anointing of ease shall rest upon your life today. Grace makes you function without struggles. As of today, no more struggle, no more hardship for you.

Grace is the divine ability to start and complete a God-given task in spite of opposition, obstacles, and adversity. Anointing for completion falls on you now in Jesus' name. Grace is an unmerited favour. Blessings you did not deserve, goodness you didn't labor for shall locate you this season in Jesus' name.

Grace is one way God makes up for our shortcomings. God wants us to share His grace with others, for them to taste and see that the Lord is good. God wants us to be generous and live a holy life with His grace given to us.

When you have prayed, fasted, and tried without measuring up to standard, then it is time to fall back on His grace. Grace is in action at those times when the Holy Spirit helps us. To pray in accordance with God's will, when we do not know how to pray. (Romans 8:26, 27)

With grace, your lack, limitations, and defects are fully covered. Grace has a voice, when it sounds, all the earth shall hear. When it speaks, everyone everywhere will know about it. Grace can announce your talents/skills and make the world know about your services and products.

The only enemy of grace is sin.

What shall we say then? Shall we continue in sin, that grace may abound? God forbid. How shall we, that are dead to sin, live any longer therein?

Romans 6:1, 2

Grace is the secret behind the success of every minister, church, and individual. In 1 Corinthians 15:9-10, Apostle Paul says:

For I am the least of the apostles, that am not meet to be called an apostle, because I persecuted the church of God. But by the grace of God I am what I am: and his grace which was bestowed upon me was not in vain; but I laboured more abundantly than they all: yet not I, but the grace of God which was with me.

For the LORD God is a sun and shield: the LORD will give grace and glory: no good thing will he withhold from them that walk uprightly.

Psalms 84:11

We must acknowledge grace so that we will not suffer failure in life.

For the grace of God that bringeth salvation hath appeared to all men.

Titus 2:11

Indeed, to make Heaven is by God's grace. Grace gives us salvation. Without grace no salvation.

For by grace are ye saved through faith; and that not of yourselves: it is the gift of God:

Ephesians 2:8

GRACE DIMENSION

For all things are for your sakes, that the abundant grace might through the thanksgiving of many redound to the glory of God.

2 Corinthians 4:15

- **Abundant Grace**

And by their prayer for you, which long after you for the exceeding grace.
2 Corinthians 9:14

- **Exceeding Grace**

And the grace of our Lord was exceeding abundant with faith and love which is in Christ Jesus.
1 Timothy 1:14

- **Exceeding Abundant Grace**

That in the ages to come he might shew the exceeding riches of his grace in his kindness toward us through Christ Jesus.
Ephesians 2:7

- **Exceeding Rich Grace**

For by grace are ye saved through faith; and that not of yourselves: it is the gift of God:

Ephesians 2:8

- **Saving Grace**

And he said unto me, My grace is sufficient for thee: for my strength is made perfect in weakness. Most gladly therefore will I rather glory in my infirmities, that the power of Christ may rest upon me.

2 Corinthians 12:9

- **Sufficient Grace**

Grace and peace be multiplied unto you through the knowledge of God, and of Jesus our Lord,

2 Peter 1:2

- **Multiplying Grace**

But grow in grace, and in the knowledge of our Lord and Saviour Jesus Christ. To him be glory both now and forever. Amen.

2 Peter 3:18

- **Growing Grace**

Growing in grace is a covenant requirement to increase in the glory of God. God wants us to be progressive by growing in Grace.

But the path of the just is as the shining light, that shineth more and more unto the perfect day.
Proverbs 4:18

We scale new heights as we grow in grace. Exceptional grace is the ability or grace to grow and increase in grace. We cannot fulfill our destiny and purpose in life without growing in grace.

STEPS TO GROW IN GRACE

- Commit To Righteousness-Lifestyle

We must be committed to fearing God. Grace cannot grow with sin

Ye [are] witnesses, and God [also], how holily and justly and unblameably we behaved ourselves among you that believe:
1 Thessalonian 2:10

- Commit to the Increase in the Knowledge of God's Word

Let the elders that rule well be counted worthy of double honour, especially they who labour in the word and doctrine.
1 Timothy 5:17

- We Must Commit to the Lifestyle of Meekness

The meek will he guide in judgment: and the meek will he teach his way.
Psalms 25:9

- We Must Commit to Growing in Love for God

For I am persuaded, that neither death, nor life, nor angels, nor principalities, nor powers, nor things present, nor things to come, Nor height, nor depth, nor any other creature, shall be able to separate us from the love of God, which is in Christ Jesus our Lord.
Romans 8:38-39

- Be Committed to a Lifestyle of Obedience to Every Instruction

I can of mine own self do nothing: as I hear, I judge: and my judgment is just; because I seek not mine own will, but the will of the Father which hath sent me.

John 5:30

- Be Committed to Maintaining a Good Conscience at all Times

Maintain goodwill every time. Don't quench your conscience. God gave you your conscience to serve as a guide for you so that you will not miss your way in your quest for righteousness.

Holding faith, and a good conscience; which some having put away concerning faith have made shipwreck:
1 Timothy 1:19

- Be Committed to Lifestyle of Joy

This lifestyle keeps the grace flowing evermore. Sadness takes joy away from you.

The vine is dried up, and the fig tree languisheth; the pomegranate tree, the palm tree also, and the apple tree, even all the trees of the field, are withered: because joy is withered away from the sons of men.
Joel 1:12

- Be Committed to Building Your Faith

For by grace are ye saved through faith; and that not of yourselves: it is the gift of God:
Ephesians 2:8

Be very committed to building your faith. Don't be complacent. From little faith, move to great faith, then very great faith and before the realm of exceeding faith. The level of exceedingly faith must be your goal as a Christian desirous of walking in grace.

- Be Committed to Lifestyle of Selfless Stewardship

And ye shall serve the LORD your God, and he shall bless thy bread, and thy water; and I will take sickness away from the midst of thee. There shall nothing cast their young, nor be barren, in thy land: the number of thy days I will fulfil.
Exodus 23:25-26

- Commit to Lifestyle of Witnessing (Soul Winning)

The fruit of the righteous is a tree of life; and he that winneth souls is wise.
Proverbs 11:30

Soul willing is a command from our lord Jesus. Don't despise it. You need to be tireless in reaching out to the lost soul and those who have backslidden.

- Commit to Lifestyle of Giving & Sowing

But this I say, He which soweth sparingly shall reap also sparingly; and he which soweth bountifully shall reap also bountifully.
Every man according as he purposeth in his heart, so let him give; not grudgingly, or of necessity: for God loveth a cheerful giver. And God is able to make all grace abound toward you; that ye, always having all sufficiency in all things, may abound to every good work:
2 Corinthians 9:6-8

- Commit to a Lifestyle of Prayer

Rejoicing in hope; patient in tribulation; continuing instant in prayer; Distributing to the necessity of saints; given to hospitality.
Romans 12:12 -13

I hereby declare and legislate into your life that:

1. The Grace of God upon you will speak like never before in Jesus' name.
2. The Grace of God upon your life will not be corrupted in Jesus' name.
3. The Grace of God upon your work, home, and business

will announce you in Jesus' name.

4. When Grace spoke upon Joseph, his destiny/glory was announced, he became a Prime Minister in Egypt, I decree that your star will shine and you will be enthroned by the blood of Jesus.
5. In the name of Jesus Christ...

- receive grace for timely help in Jesus' name – Psalm 46:1
- receive grace to avoid judgment and calamity – Genesis 6:8
- receive grace for distinction and outstanding success
- receive grace that rewards labor with good result – 1 Corinthians 15:10
- receive grace to succeed where others fail.
- receive grace to reap where others had sown – John 4:3
- receive grace for your word to be accepted and honoured
- receive grace to give and receive in multitude folds
- receive grace for sufficiency at all times
- receive grace for honor and respect
- receive grace to be recognized for good
- receive grace for open doors
- receive grace to start and finish well
- receive grace to recover your losses
- receive grace to bounce back
- receive grace for security and protection
- receive grace for long life and sound health
- receive grace to pull down your mountains of difficulty
- receive grace to do well in life and be fruitful
- receive grace to overcome and arise to shine
- receive grace to finish well, finish strong and finish excellently

Prayers

1. The grace of God will announce me this year in Jesus' name.
2. The grace of God will advertise me in Jesus' name.
3. The grace of God will package me in Jesus' name.
4. The grace of God will open doors for me in Jesus' name.
5. The grace of God will break protocol for my sake in Jesus' name.
6. The grace of God will showcase me in Jesus' name.
7. The grace of God will connect me to high places in Jesus' name.
8. The grace of God will make me relevant in Jesus' name.
9. The grace of God will deliver my testimonies to me in Jesus' name.
10. The grace of God; open my heavens in Jesus' name.
11. The grace of God; make me hear good news in Jesus' name.
12. The grace of God will protect me and my family in Jesus' name.
13. The grace of God; shield and secure me and my family in Jesus' name.
14. The grace of God will prosper my work/businesses in Jesus' name.
15. The grace of God; journey with me and my family in Jesus' name.

8.

OPERATING IN THE REALM OF EXCEPTIONAL GLORY

There is one glory of the sun, and another glory of the moon, and another glory of the stars: for one star differeth from another star in glory.

1 Corinthians 15:41

Rain of abundance is also the realm of glory. Glory destroys shame and drought. Before we go further, let's start with the meaning of glory. Glory is your destiny, talent, manifestation, beauty, light, signs & wonders, originality, real you, brightness, skills, voice, peculiar strength, unique purpose, divine gift, etc.

Your glory stands as your purpose in the land of the living. Your glory is the announcement of your career and divine inheritance.

So, what is exceptional glory?

- It is Glory that Carry Honour

Glory and honour are in his presence; strength and gladness are in his place.
1 Chronicles 16:27

- Glory With Grace

For the LORD God is a sun and shield: the LORD will give grace and glory: no good thing will he withhold from them that walk uprightly.
Psalms 84:11

And the Word was made flesh, and dwelt among us, (and we beheld his glory, the glory as of the only begotten of the Father,) full of grace and truth.
John 1:14

- Glory with Favour

For thou art the glory of their strength: and in thy favour our horn shall be exalted.
Psalms 89:17

- Glory with Goodness & Mercy

Surely goodness and mercy shall follow me all the days of my life: and I will dwell in the house of the LORD forever.
Psalms 23:6

- Glory that is Making Impacts

- Glory with Relevancies

This beginning of miracles did Jesus in Cana of Galilee, and manifested forth his glory; and his disciples believed on him.
John 2:11

- Glory with Light and Enlightening Others

Arise, shine; for thy light is come, and the glory of the LORD is risen upon thee.
Isaiah 60:1

Then shall thy light break forth as the morning, and thine health shall spring forth speedily: and thy righteousness shall go before thee; the glory of the LORD shall be thy rereward.
Isaiah 58:8

Ye are the light of the world. A city that is set on an hill cannot be hid. Neither do men light a candle, and put it under a bushel, but on a candlestick; and it giveth light unto all that are in the house.

Let your light so shine before men, that they may see your good works, and glorify your Father which is in heaven.

Matthew 5:14-16

- Glory with Wonders

I am as a wonder unto many; but thou art my strong refuge.

Psalm 71:7

Behold, I and the children whom the LORD hath given me are for signs and for wonders in Israel from the LORD of hosts, which dwelleth in mount Zion.

Isaiah 8:18

Shall thy wonders be known in the dark? and thy righteousness in the land of forgetfulness?

Psalms 88:12

Then said Jesus unto him, Except ye see signs and wonders, ye will not believe.

John 4:48

- Glory with Open Heaven

Drip down, O heavens, from above, And let the clouds pour

down righteousness; Let the earth open up and salvation bear fruit, And righteousness spring up with it. I, the Lord, have created it.
Isaiah 45:8

- Glory with Divine Endorsement

When a man's ways please the Lord, He makes even his enemies to be at peace with him.
Proverbs 16:7

The steps of a good man are ordered by the Lord, and He delights in his way. Though he fall, he shall not be utterly cast down; for the Lord upholds him with His hand.
Psalm 37:23-24

- Glory with Divine Announcement and Empowerment

Now when all the people were baptized, it came to pass, that Jesus also being baptized, and praying, the heaven was opened, And the Holy Ghost descended in a bodily shape like a dove upon him, and a voice came from heaven, which said, Thou art my beloved Son; in thee I am well pleased.
Luke 3:21-22

There is one glory of the sun, and another glory of the moon,

and another glory of the stars: for one star differeth from another star in glory.
1 Corinthians 15:41

- Glory to Arise and Shine

Arise, shine; for thy light is come, and the glory of the LORD is risen upon thee. For, behold, the darkness shall cover the earth, and gross darkness the people: but the LORD shall arise upon thee, and his glory shall be seen upon thee.
And the Gentiles shall come to thy light, and kings to the brightness of thy rising.
Isaiah 60:1-3

Confess the following:
My life, arise and ...

- ü manifest new glory
- ü manifest special glory
- ü manifest glory of increase
- ü manifest glory of enlightenment
- ü manifest glory of expectations
- ü manifest glory of fruitfulness
- ü manifest glory of breakthrough
- ü manifest glory of blessings
- ü manifest glory of prosperity
- ü manifest glory of honour
- ü manifest glory of righteousness
- ü outstanding glory

- ü glory that stands out
- ü excellent glory
- ü awakening glory

Awake up, my glory; awake, psaltery and harp: i myself will awake early. (until your glory awake , you will be sleeping .

Psalms 57:8

- Glory with Rejoicing

Therefore my heart is glad, and my glory rejoiceth: my flesh also shall rest in hope.

Psalms 16:9

I decree that your glory will not be mourned in Jesus' name. Your glory shall not be sad or sorrowful in Jesus' name.

Let the saints be joyful in glory: let them sing aloud upon their beds.

Psalms 149:5

I pray that your glory will continue to rejoice in Jesus' name. It will sing praises and your destiny, and glory shall not be crippled in Jesus' name. You shall not be captured in Jesus' name and the arrow of wasters fired at your finance, and glory shall backfire in Jesus name.

My people are destroyed for lack of knowledge: because thou hast rejected knowledge, I will also reject thee, that thou shalt be no priest to me: seeing thou hast forgotten the law of thy God, I will also forget thy children.

As they were increased, so they sinned against me: therefore will I change their glory into shame.

Hosea 4:6-7

Why You Need Exceptional Glory

Arise, shine; for thy light is come, and the glory of the LORD is risen upon thee. For, behold, the darkness shall cover the earth, and gross darkness the people: but the LORD shall arise upon thee, and his glory shall be seen upon thee. And the Gentiles shall come to thy light, and kings to the brightness of thy rising.

Isaiah 60:1-3

You are not created to be a common man. You should be exceptional. You are created for exceptional glory. Your life must display the greatness and richness embedded in the kingdom of God.

Nonetheless, you must understand that your glory must be refreshed always by God, because he is a lifter of your head and glory.

Saying with a loud voice, Worthy is the Lamb that was slain to receive power, and riches, and wisdom, and strength, and honour, and glory, and blessing.

Revelation 5:12

Exceptional glory will give you power, riches, wisdom, strength, blessings, etc.

Why Your Glory Needs Deliverance and Anointing

- *The Enemies Try to Tame People's Glory*

And delivered his strength into captivity, and his glory into the enemy's hand.
Psalms 78:61

I command your glory to come out of the hands of the enemies in Jesus' name.

- *Glory Can Fly Away*

As for Ephraim, their glory shall fly away like a bird, from the birth, and from the womb, and from the conception.
Hosea 9:11

- *Glory Can Be Turned To Shame*

O ye sons of men, how long will ye turn my glory into shame? how long will ye love vanity, and seek after leasing? Selah.
Psalms 4:2

A reproached glory cannot rejoice. So, you need deliverance

and anointing for your glory, so that it will not be turned to shame.

- *Glory Can Be Reduced*

And in that day it shall come to pass, that the glory of Jacob shall be made thin, and the fatness of his flesh shall wax lean.
Isaiah 17:4

- *Glory Can Be Silent*

To the end that my glory may sing praise to thee, and not be silent. O LORD my God, I will give thanks unto thee forever.
Psalms 30:12

- *Glory Can Be Changed to Animal Life, Or Caged*

Thus they changed their glory into the similitude of an ox that eateth grass.
Psalms 106:20

- *Glory Can Be Stripped Away*

He hath stripped me of my glory, and taken the crown from my head.
Job 19:9

- *Family Godly Glory Can be Stolen by Family Task Master*

And he heard the words of Laban's sons, saying, Jacob hath taken away all that was our father's; and of that which was our father's hath he gotten all this glory.
Genesis 31:1

- *Glory Can Be Delivered Into Captivity*

And delivered his strength into captivity, and his glory into the enemy's hand.
Psalms 78:61

- *Glory Can Be Made to Cease from Functioning*

Thou hast made his glory to cease, and cast his throne down to the ground.
Psalms 89:44

- *Many Are Going About With Unprofitable Glory*

Hath a nation changed their gods, which are yet no gods? but my people have changed their glory for that which doth not profit.
Jeremiah 2:11

- *Glory Can Be Spoiled*

There is a voice of the howling of the shepherds; for their glory is spoiled: a voice of the roaring of young lions; for the pride of Jordan is spoiled.
Zechariah 11:3

- *Glory Can Be Filled With Shame*

Thou art filled with shame for glory: drink thou also, and let thy foreskin be uncovered: the cup of the LORD'S right hand shall be turned unto thee, and shameful spewing shall be on thy glory.
Habakkuk 2:16

Also, note that ...

- Glory can be destroyed or wasted
- Glory can be damaged
- Glory can be castrated
- Glory can be terminated

- Glory can be buried
- Glory can be crippled
- Glory can be bewitched or manipulated into error and mistake
- They can empty glory
- They put off the light of glory
- Glory can be poisoned
- Glory can be deformed
- Glory can be delayed or stagnated
- Glory can be pegged
- Glory can depart
- Glory can be diverted
- Glory can be exchanged
- Glory can be hindered
- Glory can be paralyzed
- Glory can be crawling or dragging on the floor
- Glory be can drowned
- Glory can be idle in the market of life
- Glory can be sleeping or dosing
- Glory can be useless
- Hell can swallow glory (many glories have descended into hell)

Therefore, hell hath enlarged herself, and opened her mouth without measure: and their glory, and their multitude, and their pomp, and he that rejoiceth, shall descend into it.

Isaiah 5:14

Biblical Examples

- Jesus manifested glory

This beginning of miracles did Jesus in Cana of Galilee, and manifested forth his glory; and his disciples believed on him.
John 2:11

- Joseph manifested glory

He was determined, focused, and full of holiness and kindness. Read the story in Genesis 37.

- Esther manifested glory

Her relationship with the right mentor helped her to manifest glory. Read accounts in Esther 1, 2, and 3.

- Jabez manifested glory

He cried against his wrong foundation. I Chronicles 4:9-10.

- Esau

Esau regained his first-born glory back. Genesis 33:9

- Samson

Unfortunately, Samson lost his glory on the lap of Delilah. Judges 16:16-21.

- Eli

Eli lost his old-family glory. 1 Samuel 4.

- Naboth

He lost his good family-inherited glory to Jazebel's witchcraft attack. I King 21.

- Judas

A lot of people are familiar with the story of Judas who lost eternal glory because of greed. Math 27:3-5, Act 1:23-26.

Glory Restoration Key
Know this today: Life without God is an empty glory.

For the lord god is a sun and shield: the lord will give grace and glory: no good thing will he withhold from them that walk uprightly.

Psalms 84:11

The righteous shall be glad in the lord, and shall trust in him; and all the upright in heart shall glory.

Psalms 64:10

Jesus is the ...

- King of glory
- Giver of glory
- Glory builder
- Glory decorator
- Glory adjusters
- Glory sustainer
- Glory provider
- Glory potter
- Glory restorer
- Glory lifter
- Glory promoter
- Glory announcer
- Glory beautifier
- Glory enlarger
- Glory empoweree
- Glory strengthener
- Glory endorsers

Dear readers, the King of glory is calling you, to give your life to Jesus. Walk in his ways. Commit your glory and life to him. Your glory will rejoice again in Jesus name.

Say this prayer:

Lord Jesus, I confess my sins and ask for your forgiveness. Please come into my heart as my Lord and Savior. Take complete control of my life and help me to walk in Your

footsteps daily by the power of the Holy Spirit. Thank you, Lord for saving me and for answering my prayer.

Prophetic Declarations

I declare in accordance with the scriptures that...

- God will refresh your glory

My glory was fresh in me, and my bow was renewed in my hand.

Job 29:20

- God will begin to defend your glory in Jesus' name

And the lord will create upon every dwelling place of mount zion, and upon her assemblies, a cloud and smoke by day, and the shining of a flaming fire by night: for upon all the glory shall be a defence.

Isaiah 4:5

- You shall be raised up in glory in Jesus' name

It is sown in dishonour; it is raised in glory: it is sown in weakness; it is raised in power:

1 Corinthians 15:43

- By divine order, global glory is your inheritance as from today in Jesus' name

The wise shall inherit glory: but shame shall be the promotion of fools.
Proverbs 3:35

- God will empower your glory to be recognized as from today in Jesus' name

To see thy power and thy glory, so as i have seen thee in the sanctuary.
Psalms 63:2

- Let your goodly and Godly family glory be restored in Jesus' name

And they shall hang upon him all the glory of his father's house, the offspring and the issue, all vessels of small quantity, from the vessels of cups, even to all the vessels of flagons.
Isaiah 22:24

- Your glory shall receive global impart and announcement in Jesus' name

And ye shall tell my father of all my glory in egypt, and of all that ye have seen; and ye shall haste and bring down my father hither.

Genesis 45:13

- You will begin to appear in glory in Jesus' name

When the lord shall build up zion, he shall appear in his glory.

Psalms 102:16

- Your glory will not be caged anymore in Jesus' name

To see thy power and thy glory, so as i have seen thee in the sanctuary.

Psalms 63:2

- Your glory will rejoice and be glad in Jesus' name

The righteous shall be glad in the lord, and shall trust in him; and all the upright in heart shall glory.

Psalms 64:10

Pitfalls of Glory

- Sin

My people are destroyed for lack of knowledge: because thou hast rejected knowledge, i will also reject thee, that thou shalt be no priest to me: seeing thou hast forgotten the law of thy god, I will also forget thy children.

As they were increased, so they sinned against me: therefore will i change their Glory to shame

Hosea 4:6

- Lack of spiritual knowledge
- Wrong environment
- Wrong relationship
- Evil or polluted foundation
- Incomplete deliverance
- Lack of genuine and strong spiritual covering

Glory Restoration Prayers

1. Thank you, King of glory.
2. Anointing for exceptional glory, rest upon me now in the name of Jesus Christ.
3. The mercy of God, search out my glory for restoration in Jesus' name.
4. Heaven, open upon my glory for manifestation in Jesus' name.
5. My glory, arise and shine In Jesus' name.
6. My destiny, my glory from any captivity, from any bondage, escape now in Jesus' name.

7. Family altar holding my glory down, scatter by fire in Jesus' name.
8. Family darkness covering my glory, fade away now in Jesus' name.
9. Ancestral prison of limitation, affecting my greatness and progress catch fire and let me go in Jesus' name.
10. Any family taskmaster trading with my glory and virtue, release me and die in Jesus' name.
11. My glory rejects death and tragedy in Jesus' name.
12. My glory rejects problem or any crisis in Jesus' name.
13. Thou vehicle of my destiny, reject backwardness in Jesus' name.
14. My glory, reject set back In Jesus' name.
15. My glory, reject casualty In Jesus' name.
16. Activities of darkness against my glory, scatter by fire in Jesus' name.
17. Dream attacks against my glory, be canceled in Jesus' name.
18. Arrow of darkness fired at my glory, jump out and go back to the sender in Jesus' name.
19. Negative words ever spoken to my glory, backfire in Jesus' name.
20. My glory, my glory, my glory, begin to make impacts in Jesus' name.

9.

ANOINTING FOR SUPERNATURAL INCREASE

I will also save you from all your uncleannesses: and i will call for the corn, and will increase it, and lay no famine upon you.

Ezekiel 36:29

What is supernatural increase? Let us look at scriptural perspectives before we delve deeper: *And Jesus increased in wisdom and stature, and in favor with God and ma"* – Luke 2:52. *And he increased his people greatly, and made them stronger than their enemies.* – Psalms 105:24. Supernatural increase is the help from above that changes your status, position, level, and influence. It is divine help that turnaround your life for massive increase.

For the seed shall be prosperous; the vine shall give her fruit, and the ground shall give her increase, and the heavens shall give their dew; and I will cause the remnant of this people to possess all these things.

Zechariah 8:12

Words denoting increase are, Multiplication, enlargement, expansion, greatness, fruitfulness, etc. Supernatural increase gives birth to dominion, which helps you to subdue, take territory, and have an impact. Indeed, it is a sign of fulfilling God's agenda and promises. Supernatural increase that carries comfort and safety is yours this year and beyond in Jesus name.

The Lord shall increase you more and more, you and your children.
Psalm 115: 14

Increase unlimited is your portion in Jesus name.

Though thy beginning was small, yet thy latter end should greatly increase.
Job 8:7

Forget about your small beginnings. Forget about how you started. God will increase you in Jesus name. God will enlarge you in Jesus name. God will expand you in Jesus name. God will multiply you in Jesus name. God will make you exceedingly great in Jesus name.

Yea, the lord shall give that which is good; and our land shall yield her increase.
Psalm 85:12

Your land will release good increase unto you in Jesus name.

And sow the fields, and plant vineyards, which may yield fruits of increase. He blesseth them also, so that they are multiplied greatly; and suffereth not their cattle to decrease.
Psalms 107:37, 38

Your investment shall yield increase. You shall not suffer decrease anymore.

And out of them shall proceed thanksgiving and the voice of them that make merry: and i will multiply them, and they shall not be few; i will also glorify them, and they shall not be small.
***Jeremiah* 30:19**

No more reductions. No more limits. No more lack. No more scarcity of good things in your life.

Impact of Supernatural Increase

Supernatural increase breaks the backbone of lack and poverty.

Then shall he give the rain of thy seed, that thou shalt sow the ground withal; and bread of the increase of the earth, and it shall be fat and plenteous: in that day shall thy cattle feed in large pastures."
Isaiah 30:23

Supernatural Increase Bring Enlargement

For the seed shall be prosperous; the vine shall give her fruit, and the ground shall give her increase, and the heavens shall give their dew; and i will cause the remnant of this people to possess all these things."

Zechariah 8:12

Supernatural Increase Brings Prosperity

Thus saith the lord god; I will yet for this be enquired of by the house of israel, to do it for them; i will increase them with men like a flock.

Zechariah 36:37

Supernatural Increase Will Make You to Flourish

And the tree of the field shall yield her fruit, and the earth shall yield her increase, and they shall be safe in their land, and shall know that i am the lord, when i have broken the bands of their yoke, and delivered them out of the hand of those that served themselves of them.

Ezekiel 34:27

Brethren, I decree over you that supernatural increase that come with safety shall be yours this year and beyond in Jesus name.

And the Lord make you to increase and abound in love one toward another, and toward all men, even as we do toward you.

1 Thessalonian 3:12

And he increased his people greatly; and made them stronger than their enemies.

Psalm 105:24

Points to Note about Supernatural Increase

1. Supernatural increase is given by God

I planted, apollo watered but god gave the increase. So then neither he who plants is anything nor he who waters but god who gives the increase
***1 Corinthians* 3:6, 7**

2. God almighty is progressive

- God is the giver of increase.
- God alone can release increase.
- God is the distributor of increase.
- God is the custodian and controller of increase.
- God is the one who rewards efforts with increase.
- God warehouses increase and gives it as he wills.

God will favor you with abundant increase in Jesus name. You need to know that the supernatural must attend to your efforts and labor before you see an increase.

Except the lord builds the house, they labour in vain that build it: except the lord keep the city, the watchman waketh but in vain.
***Psalm* 127:1**

When God breathes upon that labour, it brings out bountiful increase. It brings the supernatural that makes increase well and perfect one.

Every good gift and every perfect gift is from above, and cometh down from the father of lights, with whom is no variableness, neither shadow of turning.
James 1:17

3. Supernatural increase comes when a seed is planted

For even when we were with you, we commanded you this; if anyone will not work, neither shall he eat.
2 Thessalonian 3:10

While the earth remains, seedtime and harvest, cold and heat, winter and summer, and day and night shall not cease.
Genesis 8:22

Learn to invest. Learn to sow. Supernatural turn small seeds into great increase. You need to start something somewhere today.

Though thy beginning was small, yet thy latter end should greatly increase.
Job 8:7

Don't despise the days of small beginnings. Great things start small. And then you need to discover your purpose in life in order to move into the realm of supernatural increase of harvest.

4. The supernatural will give you ideas for increase

In the realm of the supernatural, you will get ideas for increase in all your endeavors. Simply, ask the Holy Spirit for uncommon ideas & insight. You will surely get it.

I will instruct thee and teach thee in the way which thou shalt go: I will guide thee with mine eye.
Psalm 32:8

Don't be idle. Don't be lazy. Don't let your age be your cage or barrier. It is never late to start something. History books are replete with stories of those who founded great companies when they are old.

You need to also know that godliness, integrity and industry will enhance your increase. Achievers are hard workers and great thinkers. Supernatural increase comes when you know that you are more than your present level.

And amaziah said to the man of god, but what shall we do for the hundred talents which i have given to the army of israel? And the man of god answered, the lord is able to give thee much more than this.
2 Chronicles 25: 9

There is an anointing of "I have more than enough". Receive it now in Jesus name. There is an anointing of "having much more than this"; receive it in Jesus name. By all means, if you want to see increase, don't be complacent. Strive for more. Go for more. Ask God for more. Our God is not tired of blessing people, he would open the windows of heaven over you, again and again.

5. Supernatural increase is generational

The lord shall increase you more and more, you and your children.
Psalm 115:14

Your increase must affect the oncoming generations. The increase is beyond you. Your children must also increase and their off-springs generationally.

6. Supernatural increase come along with comfort

Thou shalt increase my greatness, and comfort me on every side.
Psalm 71:21

Your greatness is unlimited, don't limit the increase by your mindset and behaviour. God is increasing it absolutely. Your increase comes along with comfort on every side. This means that you will testify of this kind of increase in your generation.

To experience generational increase, you must embark daily on self-development and research.

7. Supernatural increase may be affected by your location

Where you reside may determine your level of supernatural increase. Let's look at the biblical examples of Abraham and Isaac:

- Abraham

Now the lord had said unto Abram, get thee out of thy country, and from thy kindred, and from thy father's house, unto a land that i will shew thee: And I will make of thee a great nation, and i will bless thee, and make thy name great; and thou shalt be a blessing: And I will bless them that bless thee, and curse him that curseth thee: and in thee shall all families of the earth be blessed.

Genesis 12:1-3

For instance, when Abraham was directed to his land of increase by God, he prospered in his new location. Always allow God to direct you to your place of increase. God is a wise investor; he won't increase you in the wrong location. Your neighborhood, business premises, place of worship; the country you are living in, will determine the level of your increase.

- Isaac

And there was a famine in the land, beside the first famine that was in the days of Abraham. And Isaac went unto Abimelech king of the philistines unto Gerar. And the lord appeared unto him, and said, go not down into Egypt; dwell in the land which i shall tell thee of: Sojourn in this land, and i will be with thee, and will bless thee; for unto thee, and unto thy seed, I will give all these countries, and i will perform the oath which I sware unto Abraham thy father; Then Isaac sowed in that land, and received in the same year an hundredfold: and the lord blessed him. And the man waxed great, and went forward, and grew until he became very great:

Genesis 26:1– 3, 12 & 13

Isaac had mighty yields because of his obedience to relocate to the place commanded. May you be guided to your place of increase in Jesus name.

I will instruct thee and teach thee in the way which thou shalt go: I will guide thee with mine eye.

Psalm 32:8

8. Fervent prayer provokes supernatural increase

Confess your faults one to another, and pray one for another, that ye may be healed. The effectual fervent prayer of a righteous man availeth much.

James 5:16

And jabez was more honourable than his brethren: and his mother called his name jabez, saying, because i bare him with sorrow.
1 Chronicles 4:9

And Jabez called on the God of Israel, saying, oh that thou wouldest bless me indeed, and enlarge my coast, and that thine hand might be with me, and that thou wouldest keep me from evil, that it may not grieve me! And god granted him that which he
1 Chronicles 4:10

9. Strong faith triggers supernatural increase

Through faith also Sara herself received strength to conceive seed, and was delivered of a child when she was past age, because she judged him faithful who had promised.
Hebrews 11:11

Why supernatural increase? You need supernatural increase because all your attempts in the remaining days of your life must end in progress and not difficulties. The situation must not stand still in your life.

There must be more meaningful success in your life. So that people will not oppress you with their personality, capacity, potentiality, and connections.

How to Access Great Increase

1. Let God always dwell in your home

In II Samuel 6:11, the ark of the Lord was in the house of Obed-Edom. The ark here signifies the presences of God. The presence of God matters in all areas of your life. When God dwells in your life, he will establish his covenant of multiplication with you. You will get the covenant of increase.

2. You must have faith in God

Faith is your access to great increase. Without faith, you can't receive anything from God. God is a spirit and you must be in spirit to serve him.

3. Destroy the spirit of fear

Fear is a trap of the enemy. To access great increase, you must destroy the spirit of fear. Romans 8:15. In the Bible, Esther risked her life to save the lives of the Jews. David destroyed fear to face Goliath. Joshua and Caleb were fearless.

4. Work hard and Work Smart

Don't solve laziness with prayer. Work hard. Work smart. You must work to access great increase. Genesis 26:14, Proverb 13:11, 1 Corinthians 3:3-8.

You need to work and pray because that is the best way to divine increase. No matter your age, keep sowing. Work and pray.

5. You must be a giver

Givers never lack. Lack is not in the DNA of givers because they are constantly living in the realm of great things. When you give to the poor, you loan to God and you will receive back from God in multitude. Luke 6:38, Proverb 19:17.

6. Don't dance to the enemy's music

The music of the enemy is destruction, failure and hindrance. The enemy's music is meant to discourage and bring you down. Don't believe in discouragement. Keep moving.

Prayer Against the Rage of the Enemies at Your Harvest

The enemies rage against you:

- When you are about doing well in life.
- When your settlement is to be concluded
- Whcn you arc about to movc to your ncxt lcvcl.
- When your Testimonies are very sure.
- When you are moving from minimum to Maximum.
- When you are about to be promoted.
- When your elevation is imminent.

- When your Help is so near.
- When you are at the edge of destiny changing breakthrough.
- When the prophetic agenda for your life is about manifesting.
- When that repeated yoke is about broken.
- When you are about to escape from the snare of the fowlers.
- When God is about to turn again your captivity.
- When your international doors are about to open.
- When you are about to secure your Visa or permanent residency.
- When your life is about making positive History.
- When you have a colorful destiny
- When you are dangerous to them in the dark kingdom.
- When you are about to celebrate big time.
- When you are about having explosive testimonies.
- When you are ready to cross your red sea, your Jericho to the promised

However, there is a way out. God is still in the business of setting the captive free. If the enemies are raging against you, I decree your freedom right now in Jesus name. Amen.

Why do the heathen rage, and the people imagine a vain thing? The kings of the earth set themselves, and the rulers take counsel together, against the LORD, *and against his anointed, saying,* Let *us break their bands asunder, and cast away their cords from us. He that sitteth in the heavens shall laugh: the Lord shall have them in derision.*

Then shall he speak unto them in his wrath, and vex them in his sore displeasure. Yet have I set my king upon my holy hill of Zion. I will declare the decree: the LORD hath said unto me, Thou art my Son; this day have I begotten thee. Ask of me, and I shall give thee the heathen for thine inheritance, and the uttermost parts of the earth for thy possession. Thou shalt break them with a rod of iron; thou shalt dash them in pieces like a potter's vessel.

Psalm 2:1- 9

PRAYERS

1. Heaven great increase for my tomorrow, open upon me in Jesus name.
2. Anointing of surplus in all areas of life, fall on me in Jesus name.
3. Anointing of excess, fall on me in Jesus name.
4. Anointing of overflowing increase fall on me in Jesus name.
5. Anointing of running over blessings and increase fall on me in Jesus name.
6. Anointing of sufficiency, fall on me in Jesus name.
7. Anointing of abundance, fall on me in Jesus name.
8. Anointing of 'I have more than enough', fall on me in Jesus name.
9. Father, breath great increase upon the work of my hands in Jesus name.
10. Altar of reduction, stagnation, unfruitful, fired at me, back fire in Jesus name.
11. Any embargo and siege of darkness upon my effort, be lifted in Jesus name.

12. Power wasting my great increase, be wasted this year and beyond in Jesus name.
13. I declare my roundabout great increase in Jesus name.
14. All my attempt, labour, efforts, strategies, plans, ideas and prayers shall yield great increase in Jesus name.
15. This year and beyond, in the name of Jesus, I receive......for great increase in Jesus name.

- opening heavens
- divine approval
- divine recommendation
- divine endorsement
- divine backup
- divine support

16. By supernatural increase, I shall be stronger than my all enemies this year and beyond in Jesus name.
17. Great increase shall be recorded in my family, career and job in the name of Jesus.
18. I will never be small again for the rest of my life.
19. Anyone standing against my great increase will be destroyed by the power of the Holy Spirit.
20. I shall be the head and not the tail in the name of Jesus.
21. Great increase, fall upon me now in Jesus name.
22. In this land, I will receive great increase in the name of Jesus.
23. Oh Lord my father, make me great and stronger than my enemies, in all areas, in the name of Jesus.
24. Thank you Jesus for answering my prayers.

10.

RAIN OF ABUNDANT LIFE

The thief cometh not, but for to steal, and to kill, and to destroy: I am come that they might have life, and that they might have it more abundantly.

John 10:10

God desires that his children should live a life full of greatness and blessings. I decree that by the power of God, receive financial abundance in Jesus' name. Abundant life includes divine health. Therefore, I command that you will receive the abundant life of God for good health in Jesus' name.

As you are reading this, receive the life of God in abundance that eliminates any disease in Jesus' name. By the abundant life of God, the following must disappear in Jesus' name:

- Liver problem
- Kidney problem
- Heart problem
- Digestive problem
- Cells problems
- Organ problem

- Menstrual problems
- Anus problems
- Indigestion in the stomach
- Skin problem
- Breathing problems
- Brain Problems
- Abnormal temperature
- Abnormal blood pressure
- Blood disorder
- Blood cell disorder
- Anemia, Bleeding disorder, (Hemophilia)Blood clots,
- Evil Swelling in any part of the body
- Cancer of the Kidney
- Cancer of the Lungs
- Colon cancer
- Liver cancer
- Blood cancer (leukemia)
- Breast cancer
- Prostate Cancer
- Skin cancer
- Bladder cancer
- Stomach cancer
- Intestine Cancer
- Colorectal cancer
- Kidney Stones
- Stroke Symptoms
- Strange Headache
- Skin Problems
- Evil Swelling in any part of the body
- Demonic Pile
- Fainting Attacks

- Weakness
- Diabetes
- Aging Abnormally
- Closed Wombs
- Sperm Problems
- Deadness of any part of your body
- Epilepsy
- Adult Bedwetting
- Adult Convulsion
- Tumor Evil Growth
- Fibroid
- Impotence
- Strange Libido
- Unusual Sexual Urge (Low & High)
- Abnormal Sex Organ
- Strange movement in the body disappears
- Any disease at all

I command the root of these sicknesses to DRY UP right now in Jesus' name. Amen.

The thief comes only to steal and kill and destroy; I have come that they may have life, and have it to the full.
John 10:10 (NIV)

Abundant life is about living life in line with God's purpose and plans. His plans are not evil. The plan of God is joy unlimited. When the rain of abundant life falls on your life, finance, business, career and marriage, you will flow in prosperity and live life to the fullest.

Rain of abundant life is:

- Righteousness (Right standing with God)
- Joy unlimited.
- Long life
- Business breakthrough
- Happy marriage
- Godly spouse
- Godly children
- Godly living
- Divine health
- Enough money to spend, invest and give
- Ease of supporting kingdom advancement projects
- Ease of soul winning
- Influence in your field and place of calling
- Peaceful living devoid of depression and sorrow

Dear brethren, you also can enter these real of abundant living. It is the heritage of every born-again Christian. Once you give your life to Christ, you have automatic entrance into this realm of abundant living.

You will succeed in Jesus name. Amen.

Prayers

1. Thank you, my Father, for the gift of abundant life represented by your son, Jesus Christ.
2. I decree that any limiting factor stopping me from entering into my season of abundant life will be consumed by fire right now in Jesus' name.
3. Holy Ghost fire, consume every limiting spirit pulling me back from getting into the rain of abundant life.

4. I decree that the rain of abundant life will not cease in my life in Jesus name. Amen
5. Nothing shall stop me from experiencing the fullness of my heritage in Christ.
6. In the name of Jesus, my life will exemplify the rain of abundance.
7. No more dryness in my life. Rain of joy and peace saturate me now and forever more in Jesus name.
8. Signs and wonders shall continually be my testimony in Jesus name.
9. In the name of Jesus, the rain of abundant revival to be spiritually alive will be my portion. No more spiritual dryness in my life.
10. In Jesus name, I decree that I will always create a spiritual atmosphere that will keep my heaven open for rain of abundant life.

11.

DIVINE PROVISION FOR THE NEXT LEVEL

Save now, I beseech thee, O LORD: O LORD, I beseech thee, send now prosperity.

Psalms 118:25

What is provision? Oxford Dictionary defines provision as the action of providing or supplying something for use. Not only that, provision is an amount or thing supplied or provided. A provision represents funds set aside for future expenses or other losses such as reductions in asset value.

Beloved, I wish above all things that thou mayest prosper and be in health, even as thy soul prospereth.
3 John 1:2

I decree that any amount you need for the next level, heaven will supply it all in Jesus' name. Receive spiritual provision right now. Receive marital provision. Enter into the realm of sweatless financial provision

Great Supplier

For the LORD hath chosen Zion; he hath desired it for his habitation. This is my rest for ever: here will I dwell; for I have desired it. I will abundantly bless her provision: I will satisfy her poor with bread.

Psalms 132:13-15

Then Joseph commanded to fill their sacks with corn, and to restore every man's money into his sack, and to give them provision for the way: and thus did he unto them.

Genesis 42:25

They shall be abundantly satisfied with the fatness of thy house; and thou shalt make them drink of the river of thy pleasures.

Psalms 36:8

I pray that God will fill your home with his provision for the next level in Jesus' name.

And gavest them bread from heaven for their hunger, and broughtest forth water for them out of the rock for their thirst, and promisedst them that they should go in to possess the land which thou hadst sworn to give them.

Nehemiah 9:15

And God is able to make all grace abound toward you; that ye, always having all sufficiency in all things, may abound to every good work:

2 Corinthians 9:8

Grace for Sufficient Provision

Be rest assured that there is grace for sufficient provision. All that you need will be handed unto you speedily in much measure.

But my God shall supply all your need according to his riches in glory by Christ Jesus.

Philippians 4:19

Relax! God is rich in all things; our maker is rich in provision for the next level. Don't be anxious or apprehensive.

I will abundantly bless her provision: I will satisfy her poor with bread.

Psalms 132:15

They shall not be ashamed in the evil time: and in the days of famine they shall be satisfied.

Psalms 37:19

The LORD is my shepherd; I shall not want. He maketh me to lie down in green pastures: he leadeth me beside the still waters.

Psalms 23:1-2

There is no debate when it comes to the issue of the reality of God words for divine provision. You can find the promises in every page of the scriptures.

For ye know the grace of our Lord Jesus Christ, that, though

he was rich, yet for your sakes he became poor, that ye through his poverty might be rich.
2 Corinthians 8:9

Jesus has exchanged his riches for us; so that we will not be poor anymore.

He that spared not his own Son, but delivered him up for us all, how shall he not with him also freely give us all things?
Romans 8:32

God is the giver of all good things. All you need to do is just to believe in him.

Now unto him that is able to do exceeding abundantly above all that we ask or think, according to the power that worketh in us.
Ephesians 3:20

The almighty is not bound to use a particular method for his miracle. He uses different methods. He even uses the least expected to carry out his agenda on earth.

Consider the ravens: for they neither sow nor reap; which neither have storehouse nor barn; and God feedeth them: how much more are ye better than the fowls?
Luke 12:24

It is my prayer for you that God will lead you to the place of abundant provision in Jesus' name. You will not lack any more.

Beloved, no matter your level, standard, or qualifications,

you still need provisions for the next level in life. No man has it all. There is always a need in the life of everyone. It is only God that is all-sufficient.

Again, I pray for you that you will receive divine provision for the remaining days, weeks, and months of this glorious year in Jesus name. I decree that you will receive: divine provision for the next journey; divine provision for the next level; divine provision for the next progress; divine provision for the next breakthrough; divine provision for new ideas; divine provision for the vision/dream God has deposited in you.

In Jesus name, you will receive divine provision spiritually, and physically.

Case Study 1 (Divine Provisions for Strength – Elijah)

And as he lay and slept under a juniper tree, behold, then an angel touched him, and said unto him, Arise and eat.
And he looked, and, behold, there was a cake baken on the coals, and a cruse of water at his head. And he did eat and drink, and laid him down again.
And the angel of the LORD came again the second time, and touched him, and said, Arise and eat; because the journey is too great for thee.
And he arose, and did eat and drink, and went in the strength of that meat forty days and forty nights unto Horeb the mount of God.

1 Kings 19:5 -8

In 1 Kings 19:5-8, we witness a powerful display of God's divine provision for the Prophet Elijah during a time of great need and discouragement. This passage reveals God's care and sustenance for His faithful servant.

The story unfolds with Elijah, exhausted and despondent, lying under a juniper tree. He had just experienced a tremendous victory over the prophets of Baal on Mount Carmel but was now fleeing for his life from the wrath of Queen Jezebel. In his weariness, Elijah fell into a deep sleep.

While Elijah was resting, an angel of the Lord appeared and touched him, instructing him to rise and eat. As Elijah looked around, he discovered a cake, freshly baked on hot coals, and a cruse of water placed near his head. This provision was not a mere coincidence or a lucky find–it was a divine intervention orchestrated by God Himself.

Elijah obediently partook of the food and drink provided by the angel, nourishing his body and replenishing his strength. Sustained by this heavenly provision, Elijah laid down again and fell back asleep.

However, the angel of the Lord returned a second time, once again touching Elijah and commanding him to rise and eat. The angel emphasized that the journey ahead was too great for Elijah to undertake without being strengthened through this divine nourishment.

Elijah responded to the angel's instructions, arising and partaking of the food and drink once more. This miraculous sustenance empowered him, equipping him for a forty-day and forty-night journey to Horeb, the mount of God.

God's care for Elijah goes beyond mere sustenance. It reveals His intimate knowledge of our needs, His attentiveness to our struggles, and His willingness to provide for us in unexpected and miraculous ways. The provision of food and water to Elijah demonstrates God's desire to strengthen and nourish His servants, equipping them for the journey ahead.

Just as He cared for Elijah, God cares for His people today. He is the God who sees our needs and provides for us according to His perfect plan and timing.

Case Study 2 (Divine Provision for Sustenance - Elijah & Widow Of Zarephath)

And Elijah the Tishbite, who was of the inhabitants of Gilead, said unto Ahab, As the LORD God of Israel liveth, before whom I stand, there shall not be dew nor rain these years, but according to my word.

And the word of the LORD came unto him, saying,

Get thee hence, and turn thee eastward, and hide thyself by the brook Cherith, that is before Jordan.

And it shall be, that thou shalt drink of the brook; and I have commanded the ravens to feed thee there.

So, he went and did according unto the word of the LORD: for he went and dwelt by the brook Cherith, that is before Jordan.

And the ravens brought him bread and flesh in the morning, and bread and flesh in the evening; and he drank of the brook.

And it came to pass after a while, that the brook dried up, because there had been no rain in the land.

And the word of the LORD came unto him, saying,

Arise, get thee to Zarephath, which belongeth to Zidon, and dwell there: behold, I have commanded a widow woman there to sustain thee.

So he arose and went to Zarephath. And when he came to the gate of the city, behold, the widow woman was there gathering of sticks: and he called to her, and said, Fetch me, I pray thee, a little water in a vessel, that I may drink.

And as she was going to fetch it, he called to her, and said, Bring me, I pray thee, a morsel of bread in thine hand.

And she said, As the LORD thy God liveth, I have not a cake, but an handful of meal in a barrel, and a little oil in a cruse: and, behold, I am gathering two sticks, that I may go in and dress it for me and my son, that we may eat it, and die.

And Elijah said unto her, Fear not; go and do as thou hast said: but make me thereof a little cake first, and bring it unto me, and after make for thee and for thy son.

For thus saith the LORD God of Israel, The barrel of meal shall not waste, neither shall the cruse of oil fail, until the day that the LORD sendeth rain upon the earth.

And she went and did according to the saying of Elijah: and she, and he, and her house, did eat many days.

And the barrel of meal wasted not, neither did the cruse of oil fail, according to the word of the LORD, which he spake by Elijah.

And it came to pass after these things, that the son of the woman, the mistress of the house, fell sick; and his sickness was so sore, that there was no breath left in him.

And she said unto Elijah, What have I to do with thee, O thou man of God? art thou come unto me to call my sin to remembrance, and to slay my son?

And he said unto her, Give me thy son. And he took him out of her bosom, and carried him up into a loft, where he abode, and laid him upon his own bed.

And he cried unto the LORD, and said, O LORD my God, hast thou also brought evil upon the widow with whom I sojourn, by slaying her son?

And he stretched himself upon the child three times, and cried unto the LORD, and said, O LORD my God, I pray thee, let this child's soul come into him again.
And the LORD heard the voice of Elijah; and the soul of the child came into him again, and he revived.
And Elijah took the child, and brought him down out of the chamber into the house, and delivered him unto his mother: and Elijah said, See, thy son liveth.
And the woman said to Elijah, Now by this I know that thou art a man of God, and that the word of the LORD in thy mouth is truth.

1 Kings 17:1-24

From the scripture above, we are presented with a remarkable account of God's divine provision for sustenance through the prophet Elijah. This passage showcases God's unwavering faithfulness and care for His chosen servant and those who trust in Him.

The Lord does not forsake His faithful servant, Elijah. He orchestrates events to ensure the well-being of His faithful servant. From the brook Cherith to the widow's home in Zarephath, God provides sustenance in the most unlikely of places, demonstrating His sovereignty over all circumstances.

This account also highlights the importance of faith and obedience. Both Elijah and the widow display unwavering trust in God's promises. Despite the apparent scarcity and desperate circumstances, they choose to believe and act upon God's instructions. In return, they witness the miraculous provision and faithfulness of God.

The story of God's provision for sustenance in 1 Kings 17:1-24 encourages us to place our trust in Him, even in the face of scarcity and uncertainty. It reminds us that God is the ultimate provider, capable of supplying our needs in miraculous ways. By faithfully following His instructions and relying on His faithfulness, we can experience His divine provision and care in our own lives.

When you trust in God, you are assured of divine provisions for breakthrough; divine provisions for hope and restoration; divine provisions for revival, etc.

They shall not be ashamed in the evil time: and in the days of famine they shall be satisfied.
***Psalms* 37:19**

Case Study 3 (Divine Provision for Nations through Unlikely Vessels – Four Men with Leprosy)

In the story found in 2 Kings 7:3-16, we witness a remarkable demonstration of God's ability to provide for a nation through unlikely vessels.

The city of Samaria is besieged by the Arameans, facing a severe famine that has brought the people to the brink of despair. In the midst of this crisis, four lepers, marginalized and considered outcasts in society due to their physical condition, find themselves at the city gate.

Realizing the dire situation they are in, the four lepers make a bold decision. They reasoned among themselves, acknowledging that remaining idle is equivalent to certain death. With faith and determination, they choose to venture into the camp of the Arameans, seeking a glimmer of hope for survival.

As they approach the enemy camp, they discover that God has orchestrated a miraculous turn of events. He causes the

Aramean army to hear a supernatural sound, giving them the impression of a formidable approaching army. Fear grips the Arameans, and they flee in haste, leaving behind their tents, provisions, and treasures.

The four lepers, witnessing this extraordinary provision, cannot contain their joy. They feast on abundant supplies and collect valuable resources for themselves. However, they recognize the significance of the moment. They understand that God's provision is not just for their own benefit but can extend to the entire nation.

Moved by compassion, the lepers return to Samaria and share the incredible news of God's provision with the starving population. The people rush out to the abandoned camp, gathering food, supplies, and treasures in abundance. God's provision through the unlikely vessels of the four lepers becomes a means of deliverance for the entire nation, putting an end to the famine and fulfilling His promise.

Surely, God can use the most unexpected and unlikely vessels to bring about His purposes and provide for an entire nation. In this story, four forgotten lepers, who were considered the least likely candidates for such a task, become the instruments through which God delivers His people.

The message conveyed is that God's provision transcends human limitations and societal norms. He sees the potential in those whom the world overlooks and raises them up to be agents of His provision and blessing. No doubt, God can work through anyone to accomplish His purposes and bring about miraculous provision for His people.

ENEMIES OF DIVINE PROVISIONS & PROSPERITY

God is not a man that He should lie, neither the son of man, that He should repent: hath He said, and shall He not do it? Or hath He spoken, and shall He not make it good?
Number 23:7

If you are not experiencing the fullness of the rain of abundance explained in this book, it is your fault and not God's. There are many obstacles that may stand in the way of getting to the haven of prosperity round-about. The enemy (devil) is against anything God stands for, so he would naturally constitute himself a nuisance in standing against the manifestation of a man's prosperity.

It is important to know that these enemies will stop that prosperity if we do not deal with them consciously and precisely.

The following are the enemies of provisions and prosperity:

Sin

The number one enemy of your prosperity is Sin.

Your iniquities have turned away these things and your sins have withholding good things from you.
Jeremiah 5:25

Sin devalues you. God is very intolerant of any form of iniquity. For you to prosper in your business genuinely, you must avoid sin like a plague. Don't allow sin to be around you. Repent and ask God for forgiveness.

In case you are living in sin and you want God to forgive you, say the following prayers;

Dear God,

I come before you today, acknowledging that I am a sinner in need of your forgiveness and salvation. I believe that Jesus Christ, your Son, died on the cross for my sins and rose again. I confess that Jesus is Lord and I surrender my life to Him.

Please forgive my sins, cleanse me from all unrighteousness, and fill me with your Holy Spirit. I ask for your guidance and strength to live a life that honors you. Thank you for your love, mercy, and grace.

In Jesus name, I pray. Amen.

You are now born again. You are assured of living a life full of joy and abundance.

Sexual Immorality

Flee from sexual immorality. Every other sin a person commits is outside the body, but the sexually immoral person sins against his own body

1 Corinthians 6:18

Sexual immorality has been described as a sin against one's own body. Remember the Bible also says the body of a man is the temple of the Holy Spirit and the spirit of God dwells there. 1 Corinthians 6 v 19 – 20.

So, whatever you do against your body is an infringement on the temple of the living God. Remember that your business is the work of your hands and your hands are members of your body. It is therefore safe to conclude that when you engage in sexual immorality, you are indirectly destroying your body.

Fraudulent Businesses

As the partridge sitteth on eggs and hatchet them not; so he that getteth riches, and not by right, shall leave them in the midst of his days and his end shall be a fool
Jeremiah 17:11

Everyone involved in any form of fraud will become a fool and regret it at the end of the day. No matter the investments you have done with that money, it will turn to zero. Any wealth gotten on the heels of fraud or dishonesty will not endure.

It is only the blessings of God that make a man rich without any attachment of sorrow. The way forward is to do away with your old ways and accept Jesus Christ as your Lord and Savior. Stop fraudulent practices, so that God can bless you.

Cheating

Let your business transactions and dealings be with fairness, sincerity and honesty. Cheating puts a hole in one's financial bag. Don't cheat your business partners and your workers, you won't gain anything from it.

Thou shalt not have in thy bag divers weights, a great and a small.
Thou shalt not have in thine house divers measures, a great and a small.
But thou shalt have a perfect and just weight, a perfect and just measure shalt thou have: that thy days may be lengthened in the land which the Lord thy God giveth thee."
Deuteronomy 25:13-15

Wrong Partnership

Be not deceived: evil communications corrupt good manners.
1 Corinthians 15:33

He that is surety for a stranger shall smart for it: And he that hateth suretiship is sure.
Proverbs 11:15

Wrong partnership is a great enemy of prosperity and breakthrough. A partnership acts as an incorporated business operated by two or more individuals. Once two or more individuals agree to go into business, a partnership is automatically formed.

It is very important to prayerfully consult with God before entering into any business partnership, as a wrong one could spell doom for the business.

Watch the person you are going to do business with, choose your business partners by revelation through prayers.

Repeated Negative Dreams

Negative dreams are bad enough, but a situation where the negative dreams are repeated, it may become indicative of business harvest failure.

Every negative dream should be taken seriously and dealt with appropriately. Some dreams are assigned to schedule one to uselessness and wretchedness.

Seeking Help in Egypt

Woe unto them that go down to Egypt for help; and stay on horses, and trust in Chariots, because they are many; and in horsemen, because they are very strong; but they look not unto the Holy One of Israel, neither seek the Lord"

Isaiah 31:1

Seeking help in Egypt is putting yourself and work in bondage. There is no help in Egypt, only affliction. Don't go to Egypt, you and your helpers shall both fall together. So, look up to God from whom genuine help can come. Believe in the Lord God to help you.

Laziness

He becometh poor that dealeth with a slack hand (lazy) but the hand of the diligent maketh rich laziness only gets are into poverty and lack.

Proverbs 10:4

A lazy man cannot amount to anything and prosperity will be a mirage to such. The scripture admonishes, that a lazy person should not eat. A lazy person cannot make it. Every achiever is a hard worker, and does not sleep anyhow.

Overnight Success

He that tilleth his land shall have plenty of bread: but he that followeth after vain persons shall have poverty enough. A faithful man shall abound with blessings: but he that maketh haste to be rich shall not be innocent.

Proverbs 28:19-20

Our God is a God of process, and as such, overnight success is dangerous and ungodly. Overnight success can be likened to putting papers together and setting it on fire. It generates an initial large fire that sooner than later fizzles out. Anything or success a man has not laboured for may not endure.

This is synonymous with overnight success. A quest for quick riches can never lead anyone to true prosperity. There is a process to prosperity so that your prosperity can endure.

Wrong Businesses

All that glitter is not gold. You need to carefully and prayerfully engage God in the course of entering into a business venture. You must ask God for leading into the type of business to engage in.

For the fact that some people are making it in a particular business interest, does not mean you should go into it. That others did it and prospered does not make that business the will of God for your life, so be guided by seeking the face of God through prayers.

I will instruct you and teach you in the way you should go; I will counsel you with my loving eye on you.

Psalm 32:8

Avoid the bandwagon syndrome. It is wrong to put money as your top priority ahead of God's will and what you have a passion for. Such mindset will invariably lead to taking a wrong decision which may be detrimental to your prosperity.

Wrong Location

Arise ye, and depart; for this is not your rest
Micah 2:10

Behold, I send an Angel before thee, to keep thee in the way, and to bring thee into the place which I have prepared.
Exodus 23:20

Your location is where your allocation is. Your business location really matters. Wrong spiritual location could lead to attacks on your business. A wrong location could lead to a reduction in your business, and could fight your business.

As long as you are operating in an environment where God has not ordained for you, it may be a life of sweat and struggle. So, your location is a major determinant of your prosperity, and your prosperity is a function of your divine allocation. I pray any business situated in the wrong location, let the Lord divinely relocate you in Jesus' name.

Wrong Partners/Workers

Employing the wrong workers is tantamount to inviting devourers into one's vineyard. Workers with negative mindsets on the job, especially those more interested in what they can get out of the organization and not what they can give into it.

Such workers instead of being productive, end up being counter-productive and this eventually takes its toll on the business.

Refusal to Pay Tithes

Will a man rob God? Yet ye have robbed me, But ye say,

wherein have we robbed thee? In tithes and offerings. Ye are cursed with a curse: for ye have robbed me, even this whole nation. Bring ye all the tithes into the storehouse, that there may be meat in mine house, and prove me now herewith saith the Lord of hosts, if I will not open you the windows of heaven, and pour you out a blessing, that there shall not be room enough to receive it.

Malachi 3:8–10

Refusal to pay tithes, to give offerings, to bless the servants of God, to pay your first fruits, to contribute to development in the house of God is disobedience to God's instructions and there are attendant consequences (vs 9).

For your prosperity to burst forth in whatever you do, payment of tithe is non-negotiable. A default in all of these opens or gives access to devourers to wade in. This is a great enemy of prosperity, Pay your company's tithes and also your personal income tithes.

Not Asking God for Direction

Man's goings are of the Lord; how can a man then understand his own way?

Proverbs 20:24

Not asking God for direction in any enterprise or venture is like embarking on a journey with your eyes closed, such a person is an accident going somewhere to happen. God said in Psalm 32 v 8 (if you ask me) "I will instruct thee and teach thee in the way which thou shalt go: I will guide thee with mine eye"

If you don't ask God for direction, you will operate as someone who is directionless.

Lack of Administration and Operations

Proper administration in any institution or venture can never be over-emphasized. The lack of which may stem meaningful progress therein.

GREAT SUPPLIERS

Sing the following song:

He's a great provider! He's a greater provider!
He's a great provider! He's a great provider!
He will surely provide for you and provide for me,

PRAYER

1. Father, I ask you for mercy concerning any sin I might have committed in Jesus' name.
2. O Lord my father, release your blessings for provision in Jesus' name.
3. Father, I refuse to lack any good thing in life henceforth in the name of Jesus' Christ.
4. Father, satisfy me with your goodness and fill me with your provision in Jesus' name.
5. Every enemy of my prosperity, I am no more your candidate, I reject you by fire in Jesus' name.
6. Power of God to overcome the enemies of my prosperity, fall upon me in Jesus' name.
7. O Lord, baptise me with the spirit of wisdom in my business in Jesus' name.
8. Any devourer in my business, attacking my prosperity,

your time is up, die by fire in Jesus' name.

9. Grace of God to overcome sexual immorality, fall upon me in Jesus' name.
10. I reject any fraudulent business transaction in Jesus' name.
11. Spirit of honesty and sincerity in my business transactions, envelope me in Jesus' name.
12. By fire, by force, I reject activities of strangers in my business transactions in Jesus' name.
13. Negative dreams attacking my business/prosperity, be cancelled by the blood of Jesus in Jesus' name.
14. By the strength and wisdom of God, I shall prosper in my business dealings in Jesus' name.
15. The Lord shall instruct me and lead me in the way that I should go concerning my business in Jesus' name.
16. Every agent of darkness assigned against my business/ prosperity, you are a liar, be destroyed in Jesus' name.
17. I will not labour for another to eat in Jesus' name.
18. By the mercy of God, I shall plant vineyard and I shall eat the fruit thereof in Jesus' name.
19. Distractions that can lead to business failure, O Lord my father, deliver me from them in Jesus' name.
20. Witchcraft activities/agenda programmed against my business/prosperity; you will not prosper in Jesus' name.
21. Any cloud of darkness over my business, fade away in Jesus' name.
22. I reject mistakes and errors that may cripple my business in Jesus' name.
23. By the grace of God, my business will prosper in Jesus' name.

12.

ABUNDANCE OF RAIN

And they waited for me as for the rain; and they opened their mouth wide as for the latter rain.

Job 29:23

And Elijah said unto Ahab, Get thee up, eat and drink; for there is a sound of abundance of rain.
1 Kings 18:41

Then shall he give the rain of thy seed, that thou shalt sow the ground withal; and bread of the increase of the earth, and it shall be fat and plenteous: in that day shall thy cattle feed in large pastures.
Isaiah 30:23

Mysteries of Rain

- Rain Brings About Productivity & Fruitfulness

These are the generations of the heavens and of the earth

when they were created, in the day that the LORD God made the earth and the heavens.

And every plant of the field before it was in the earth, and every herb of the field before it grew: for the LORD God had not caused it to rain upon the earth, and there was not a man to till the ground."

Genesis 2:4, 5

Nothing grows without rain. Nothing can be productive without rain. I pray for you that you will receive abundance of rain for roundabout productivity and roundabout fruitfulness in the name of Jesus.

- **Rain Brings About Watering**

In that day sing ye unto her, A vineyard of red wine. I the LORD do keep it; I will water it every moment: lest any hurt it, I will keep it night and day."

Isaiah 27:2, 3

Rain is a divine release from heaven to water the earth. Anything God waters SURVIVES, LIVES, GROWS, PRODUCES, REJOICES, and COMES ALIVE.

I pray that:

God will water your LIFE.

God will water your HEALTH.

God will water your HOME.

God will water your FAMILY.

God will water your IDEAS, VISION/ DREAM.

God will water your PREGNANCY.
God will water your BUSINESS And your WORK.
God will water your PROJECTS
God will water YOUR ENTIRE BEING in Jesus name.

- **Rain Can Lead to Overflowing Water**

He shall come down like rain upon the mown grass: as showers that water the earth.
In his days shall the righteous flourish; and abundance of peace so long as the moon endureth.
Psalms 72:6-7

In the mighty name of Jesus, you shall receive...

- Rain of abundance grace
- Rain of overflowing blessings
- Rain of overflowing capacity
- Rain of overflowing wealth
- Rain of overflowing increase
- Rain of abundance of joy
- Rain abundance of gladness
- Rain of overflowing restoration
- Rain of overflowing recovery
- Rain of overflowing testimonies
- Rain of overflowing achievement
- Rain of overflowing healing

I pray for you that:

- Your capacity and ability to produce will not reduce in life in Jesus' name.
- Your capacity and ability to do well will not reduce in life in Jesus' name.
- Your capacity and ability to excel will not reduce in life in Jesus' name.
- Your capacity and ability to achieve will not reduce in life in Jesus' name.
- Your capacity and ability to do new things will not reduce in life in Jesus' name.
- Your ability and capacity to be effective will not reduce in life in Jesus' name.
- Your ability and capacity to be competent will not reduce in life in Jesus' name.
- Your ability and capacity to succeed will not reduce in life in Jesus' name.
- Your ability and capacity to progress will not reduce in life in Jesus' name.
- Your ability and capacity to conquer territories will not reduce in life in Jesus' name.
- Your ability and capacity to prosper will not reduce in life in Jesus' name.
- Your ability and capacity to flourish will not reduce in life in Jesus name

Rain Brings Refreshing

If the clouds be full of rain, they empty themselves upon the earth: and if the tree fall toward the south, or toward the north, in the place where the tree falleth, there it shall be.

Ecclesiastics 11:3

Rain refreshes. When it rains, people feel refreshed, especially after a long time of heat waves.

I decree that your cloud that is full of rain shall rain upon you now in Jesus' name. You shall receive the rain of blessings, favour, good news in abundance, testimonies, miracles, and that of possibilities in Jesus name.

Rain Comes in Due Seasons

Then I will give you the rain for your land in its season, the early rain and the latter rain, that you may gather in your grain, your new wine, and your oil."

Deuteronomy 11:14

In your due season, I decree that you shall receive the rain of productivity, progress, achievement, abundance, increase, relevance, turnaround, knowledge, wisdom, enlargement, power, and breakthroughs that will fall on you in Jesus' name.

Rain Brings End to a Season of Drought and Dryness

And Elijah said unto Ahab, Get thee up, eat and drink; for there is a sound of abundance of rain.

1 Kings 18:41

As you receive an abundance of rain from God today, I prophesy unto you that:

- Season of Dryness
- Season of Bareness
- Season of Lack
- Season of Frustration
- Season of Disappointment
- Season of Delay
- Financial Drought & Dryness
- Marital Drought & Dryness
- Spiritual Drought & Dryness
- Any form of Drought & Dryness ... end now in Jesus' name.

Rain Makes Plants Geminate and Bring Increase

Then shall he give the rain of thy seed, that thou shalt sow the ground withal; and bread of the increase of the earth, and it shall be fat and plenteous: in that day shall thy cattle feed in large pastures.

Isaiah 30:23

Your seed shall germinate and bring out an increase. You shall receive plentiful blessings of rain. Your good and godly ideas shall geminate and bring an increase in Jesus name.

The Rain Sustains the River

And a river went out of Eden to water the garden; and from thence it was parted, and became into four heads."

Genesis 2:10

Abundance of rain for continual sustenance, receive now in Jesus' name. Rain of replenishment shall fall on you now in Jesus name Rain of divine sustenance shall fall on you in Jesus' name. Rain of continuous increase shall fall on you in Jesus' name.

Prayer Declaration

In the name of Jesus, enter into your season of abundance of rain. I decree and declare that:

- Rain of Blessings
- Rain of Fruitfulness
- Rain of Replenishment
- Rain of Subduing
- Rain of Dominion
- Rain of Increase
- Rain of Enlargement
- Rain of Spread
- Rain of New Ideas
- Rain of Creativities
- Rain of Opportunities
- Rain of Great Exploits
- Rain of Sound Health
- Rain of Progress
- Rain of Advancement
- Rain of Security
- Rain of Favour
- Rain of Mercy
- Rain of Help
- Rain of Healing

- Rain of New things
- Rain of Achievement
- Rain of Turn around
- Rain of Better life
- Rain of Lifting
- Rain of Good News
- Rain of Relevance
- Rain of Breaking New Grounds
- Rain of Abundance

...will fall on you now in Jesus' name.

Note the following:

1. **Sin Can Shut Heaven Against Rain**

When heaven is shut up, and there is no rain, because they have sinned against thee; if they pray toward this place, and confess thy name, and turn from their sin, when thou afflictest them:

1 Kings 8:35

Don't give room for sin. Always strive for righteousness. A truly righteous man is the beloved of God.

2. **Idolatry Hinders Rain**

Take heed to yourselves, that your heart be not deceived, and ye turn aside, and serve other gods, and worship them;
And then the LORD'S wrath be kindled against you, and he shut up the heaven, that there be no rain, and that the land yield not her fruit; and lest ye perish quickly from off the good land which the LORD giveth you.

Deuteronomy 11:16-17

Idolatry hinders the flow of God's rain. Don't indulge in it. Always flee from it.

3. **Not Living Holy**

And when Abram was ninety years old and nine, the LORD appeared to Abram, and said unto him, I am the Almighty God; walk before me, and be thou perfect.

Genesis 17:1

Holy living is not negotiable. You must live holy and be in the good book of God. God dwells in holiness and not in filthiness. It is therefore imperative to examine yourself on daily basis to know if you are still living a holy life.

4. **Service Triggers Abundance of Rain**

And it shall come to pass, if ye shall hearken diligently unto my commandments which I command you this day, to love the

LORD your God, and to serve him with all your heart and with all your soul,

That I will give you the rain of your land in his due season, the first rain and the latter rain, that thou mayest gather in thy corn, and thy wine, and thine oil.

Deuteronomy 11:13-14

When you serve God with all your heart and resources, heaven will surely pour down the rain of blessings upon you and the work of your hands.

5. **Be Deliberate**

Seest thou a man diligent in his business? he shall stand before kings; he shall not stand before mean men.

Proverbs 22:29

The soul of the sluggard desireth, and hath nothing: but the soul of the diligent shall be made fat.

Proverbs 13:4

Be deliberate about working hard. Plan your activities and business. Put structure in place to help you take your company to the next level.

6. **Laziness Reduces Productivity**

Go to the ant, thou sluggard; consider her ways, and be wise:
Proverbs 6:6

How long wilt thou sleep, O sluggard? when wilt thou arise out of thy sleep?
Proverbs 6:9-11

Don't be lazy. God detests laziness. Don't let laziness be found around you. Always be the one that gets things done on time.

7. **Sow Bountifully**

But this I say, He which soweth sparingly shall reap also sparingly; and he which soweth bountifully shall reap also bountifully.
Every man according as he purposeth in his heart, so let him give; not grudgingly, or of necessity: for God loveth a cheerful giver.
2 Corinthians 9:6-7

If you sow bountifully, you will receive bountifully. If you sow sparingly, you will reap sparingly. Make an attempt to sow big seeds and expect a bigger harvest.

8. **Pay Your Tithe**

Bring ye all the tithes into the storehouse, that there may be meat in mine house, and prove me now herewith, saith the LORD of hosts, if I will not open you the windows of heaven, and pour you out a blessing, that there shall not be room enough to receive it.
And I will rebuke the devourer for your sakes, and he shall not destroy the fruits of your ground; neither shall your vine cast her fruit before the time in the field, saith the LORD of hosts.
And all nations shall call you blessed: for ye shall be a delightsome land, saith the LORD of

Malachi 3:10-12

Pay your tithe promptly and always. Tithing opens the windows of heaven. When you pay your tithe, God rains abundance of blessings upon your life, family, and business.

9. **Prayers Bring Rain**

Elias was a man subject to like passions as we are, and he prayed earnestly that it might not rain: and it rained not on the earth by the space of three years and six months.
And he prayed again, and the heaven gave rain, and the earth brought forth her fruit.

James 5:17,18

Ask ye of the LORD rain in the time of the latter rain; so the LORD shall make bright clouds, and give them showers of rain, to every one grass in the field.

Zechariah 10:1

Always pray. Make prayer your daily companion. Prayer is powerful. You will receive speedy answers to your heart's desires on the altar of prayer. Do all these and see if God will not release his rain of prosperity upon you. Surely, blessings will indeed pursue and overtake you.

Prayers

1. Father, have mercy upon me wherever I have shut my heaven against my rain in Jesus' name
2. O Lord my father, release your grace for an abundance of rain upon my land (marital land, financial land, business land, spiritual land) in Jesus' name.
3. Cloud of darkness preventing my heavens to release rain, fade away in Jesus' name.
4. Any wind blowing my rain away, cease now in Jesus' name.
5. Any power diverting my rain of blessings, perish in Jesus' name
6. Rain of wonders fall upon my destiny and my household in Jesus' name.
7. Rain of testimonies, be released unto me in Jesus' name.
8. Abundance rain of blessings, fall upon me and my household in Jesus' name.
9. O yea my land, begin to yield increase for me by the help of divine rain in Jesus' name.
10. My abundant rain will not turn to a flood of sorrow and tragedy in Jesus' name.
11. My rain will not turn to sorrow and tragedy in Jesus' name.

12. Father, satisfied my soul with the rain of your goodness and make my life and home your water of blessings in Jesus' name.
13. O Lord, redeem me and everything I stand for or represent from any strong entity or personality troubling me in Jesus' name.
14. I enter into my abundance of good and glorious harvest in Jesus' name.
15. I enter into my joy unlimited in Jesus' name.
16. I enter into my divine comfort in Jesus' name.
17. I enter into my rejoicing galore in Jesus' name.
18. No more sorrow in Jesus' name.
19. Anointing for divine satisfaction falls upon me and my household in Jesus' name.

Contact

ADDRESS: 4702, Century Plaza Road, Indianapolis, Indiana, 46254, United States

PHONE NUMBER: +1317-748-5778 / +1317-701-9991

EMAIL: christspeminternational@gmail.com

WEBSITE: http://christspemchurch.org/

Made in the USA
Columbia, SC
01 December 2023